TORONTO SPRAWLS

A HISTORY

With a landmass of approximately 7,000 square kilometres and a population of roughly five million, the Greater Toronto Area is Canada's largest metropolitan centre. How did a small nineteenth-century colonial capital become this sprawling urban giant, and how did government policies shape the contours of its landscape?

In *Toronto Sprawls,* Lawrence Solomon examines the great migration from farms to the city that occurred in the last half of the nineteenth century. During this period, a disproportionate number of single women came to Toronto while, at the same time, immigration from abroad was swelling the city's urban boundaries. Labour unions were increasingly successful in recruiting urban workers in these years. Governments responded to these perceived threats with a series of policies designed to foster order. To promote single-family dwellings conducive to the traditional family, buildings in high-density areas were razed and apartment buildings banned. To discourage returning First World War veterans from settling in cities, the government offered grants to spur rural settlement. These policies and others dispersed the city's population and promoted sprawl.

An illuminating read, *Toronto Sprawls* makes a convincing case that urban sprawl in Toronto was caused not by market forces, but rather by policies and programs designed to disperse Toronto's urban population.

(University of Toronto Centre for Public Management Monograph Series on Public Policy and Public Administration)

LAWRENCE SOLOMON is an urban affairs columnist with the *National Post*, executive director of the Urban Renaissance Institute, founder and managing director of the Energy Probe Research Foundation, and a past member of the City of Toronto Planning Board.

The University of Toronto Centre for Public Management Monograph Series

Editor: Andrew Stark, University of Toronto

The University of Toronto Centre for Public Management Monograph Series is an ongoing series of books on important topical matters in public administration and public policy that will engage not only the academic community, but also policy- and opinion-makers in Canada and elsewhere.

Books are included in the series based on their originality, capacity to provoke public debate, and academic rigour.

For a list of books published in the series, see p. 121.

LAWRENCE SOLOMON

Toronto Sprawls

A History

University of Toronto Centre for Public Management Monograph Series

© University of Toronto Press Incorporated 2007
Toronto Buffalo London
Printed in Canada

Reprinted 2007

ISBN 978-0-7727-8619-7 (cloth)
ISBN 978-0-7727-8618-0 (paper)

Printed on acid-free paper

Library and Archives Canada Cataloguing in Publication

Solomon, Lawrence, 1948–
　　Toronto sprawls : a history / Lawrence Solomon.

(University of Toronto Centre for Public Management monograph series)
Includes index.
ISBN 978-0-7727-8618-0 (pbk.)
ISBN 978-0-7727-8619-7 (bound)

1. Cities and towns – Ontario – Toronto – Growth – History.　2. Toronto (Ont.) – History.　I. Title.　II. Series.

HT169.C32T67 2007　　　307.1'41609713541　　　C2007-900099-1

All rights reserved. No part of this publication may be reproduced, stored in a retrieval system, or transmitted in any form or by any means, electronic, mechanical, photocopying, recording, or otherwise, without the prior written permission of the publisher.

Printed for the University of Toronto Centre for Public Management by the University of Toronto Press.

Dedicated to Joan Berkeley Adams, my mother-in-law, for her encouragement and her many recollections and reflections on the city of her birth

Contents

Foreword ix
Preface xi
Acknowledgments xiii

Introduction: Greater Toronto, *circa* 1900, before the Era of Sprawl 3
1 How Private Transit Hobbled Sprawl 9
2 Living at Close Quarters 17
3 Toronto the Good 23
4 Model People, Model Suburbs 31
5 Canada's War Effort against the Cities 41
6 CMHC and Cheap Financing Open Up the Suburbs 50
7 Partial Amalgamation, Full Sprawl 56
　WITH SATISH DHAR
8 The Suburbs beyond the Suburbs 65
　WITH SATISH DHAR
Conclusion: How Toronto Might Have Been 72
Postscript: Toronto in 2020 79

Notes 85
Index 115

Foreword

This book will provoke almost everyone. While those on the political left will welcome Solomon's arguments that sprawl has neither an economic nor an environmental justification, they will be aghast that he puts the blame for sprawl on government rather than developers, the automobile lobby, or the other usual suspects.

Likewise, Solomon will provoke those on the political right, who in some corners have come to conclude that sprawl is actually a good thing. Most conservatives rebuff critiques of suburban life, which they find culturally wholesome and congenial. They will bristle at Solomon's claim that the tidy suburban dream, which in their mind was the creation of market forces, could not exist without concerted government intervention. And they will bridle at Solomon's claim that suburbanites, not city folk, have effectively been on the government dole.

If Solomon makes an unconventional (even unheard of) argument, he relies on the most conventional of sources – the words of the political leaders who shaped Toronto and its environs. *Toronto Sprawls* does not construct complex arguments to make its case; it merely places readers in the Toronto of one hundred years ago and of crucial decades since, exposing them to the thinking then in vogue. It reports how politicians, responding to the great reformers of the day, argued for policies that would disperse the urban population, and it details the programs that political leaders then brought in to accomplish their goals.

Solomon's many insights, which are broadly relevant to other North American urban centres, add up to one simple explanation for the cause of sprawl: governments made promises and then delivered on their promises. The upshot – Toronto grew out rather than up.

Andrew Stark
Editor, University of Toronto Centre for Public Management
Monograph Series

Preface

The automobile caused urban sprawl, claim studies in their hundreds. The development industry's lust for profits worsened sprawl, assert hundreds of others. People flocked to the suburbs for the house, yard, and fresh air they needed to raise their children, argue hundreds more. These factors, stated in academia and in the popular press, explain the historic migration from city to suburb that occurred in North America after the Second World War. People naturally wanted the suburban dream. The automobile allowed them to have it. The developers augmented these wants and profited. End of story.

And governments? They merely played a supporting role, by giving the public what it wanted. Governments aided in financing. Governments provided for roads and other infrastructure. And, in the process, governments also gave the developers and the automobile industry what they wanted. This basic story line, with minor twists in plot, characterizes most analyses of urban sprawl. Some might assign more weight to the role of developers and some more to the postwar craving for a suburban plot of one's own; some might applaud the rise of the suburbs for spreading home ownership and individualism and some might deplore suburbs for their waste and inefficiency. Many if not most of the studies lament that government did not stand up to the vested interests that promoted the suburbs, or that government did not do more to help cities during the flight of the population to the suburbs, and thus slow the cities' decline.

This basic story, I argue, is a fable. In Toronto, and undoubtedly elsewhere, governments did not play a supporting role. They took the lead role, and also directed the show. Moreover, governments acted not to satisfy the public's desires but to frustrate them. The fable persists because of a misunderstanding of the forces at play in the creation of suburbs, and false assumptions about the postwar suburb.

With the modern suburb now a fact of life, it is hard to imagine that a mere half-century ago suburbs held little status. A suburban address for most was a stigma more than a sign of success. There was no suburban dream at the close of the Second World War. With the suburban real estate industry now politically powerful, it is hard to imagine that no influential lobby then existed, when land on the outskirts of cities was held mostly by disparate farmers. Powerful real estate interests did exist – in the cities, where the industry had its investments and its expertise. The established real estate industry could be expected to resist plans to develop the suburbs and it did.

With good roads now ubiquitous and widely perceived to be an entitlement, it is hard to imagine that they weren't always present. And that automobile commuters at the end of the Second World War tended to be of modest means and very limited in their choice of residence. The automobile did, of course, become the postwar suburban vehicle of choice but it needed a driver. The unseen hand at the wheel was government, after the Second World War as after the First, when street railroads spawned suburbs and sprawl.

Governments have historically had an interest in dispersing the public. This book describes why through a short history in the life of Toronto. The story of other cities would differ little.

Acknowledgments

Satish Dhar contributed enormously to this book, co-authoring chapters 7 and 8 and providing research for others. An Ontario civil servant over the last quarter-century who helped develop many landmark pieces of legislation that now govern Ontario municipalities, Satish provided an extraordinary understanding of government policy development and decision-making.

I am also grateful for the research efforts of Carrie Elliot and Lisa Peryman, who assisted me diligently, and for the staff at the City of Toronto Archives, who were always helpful in locating documents. Patrick Kennedy, who reviewed this book prior to publication, provided insightful critiques that led to numerous improvements, as did Andrew Stark, my editor, who steered me expertly.

I also wish to thank the Empire Club of Canada, a venerable institution whose contributions to Canada I had not adequately appreciated prior to my research for this book. The Empire Club has been the venue of choice over the twentieth century for the elaboration by decision-makers of major government policy; its speakers' first-hand accounts have been indispensable in my research.

Finally, I wish to acknowledge my friend and colleague over the past three decades, Jane Jacobs. Although she did not live to see this book's completion, her influence on it has been profound.

This book has been generously supported by Community Foundation of Greater Toronto, Donner Canadian Foundation, Neptis Foundation, Margaret Laurence Fund, and McLean Foundation.

TORONTO SPRAWLS

Introduction: Toronto *circa* 1900, before the Era of Sprawl

Greater Toronto, and how best to control its growth, was in the news one hundred years ago, when the City of Toronto's northern reaches lay at Yorkville and Greater Toronto extended only four miles north of the waterfront, to Eglinton Avenue. The instinct of many of the political leaders of that era, as with many leaders in our own, was to put the growing area under the control of a streamlined government, and to expropriate privately owned utilities, in order to control the development of infrastructure. As argued in 1907 by W.F. 'Billy' Maclean, a Toronto member of the federal Parliament and a founder and editor of the *Toronto World*:

> My suggestion today is that if you speak of Greater Toronto, you must [expand the government of Toronto into the neighbouring districts] for three great public reasons. First, to control the water supply of all that country; second, to control the roads and the traction systems in that territory; third, to control the sewers and sanitation of the district. If you want a Greater Toronto, and if you want to have it right, and broad lines, and if you want to control the roads and the streets and the traction on the streets, and the water supply and the sanitation, you should make one bite of it and take in the whole Township of York.[1]

The Township of York was a one-hundred-square-mile area that ran east-west for ten miles along Lake Ontario, from the Humber River to the Don River, and ten miles north, to what has become Steeles Avenue, the city's current northern border. In effect, the Greater Toronto that Maclean championed in 1907 became a reality (and then some) in 1998, when the provincial government amalgamated the city of Toronto with its immediate suburbs.

Maclean was a leader in a heady civic reform movement that was then sweeping the country, formed to fight the private monopolies that had emerged in public transit, electricity, natural gas, telephones and other utilities. A few years earlier, the mayors of Toronto and Westmount, a Montreal suburb, had founded the Union of Canadian Municipalities to organize against monopolies that the federal and provincial governments had granted to private companies. By 1907 that movement had become broad-based and powerful, with a populist message that had great appeal to the public: 'The dispute between the municipalities and the corporate owners of the public utilities is that the corporations, becoming rich and powerful, exact from the people too high a price for what they supply and fail to give a fair and proper service for the money paid them,' summarized Toronto mayor Emerson Coatsworth, in his presidential address to the union that year.[2]

The reformers had legitimate grievances. Federal and provincial governments had often granted monopolies to well-connected corporate interests, leading to many abuses. With the monopolists not subject to competition, they faced no business pressure to reduce rates or provide better service than required by the legislation that created them. But few reformers argued that the remedy to the absence of competition lay in fostering competition, by eliminating the monopoly privileges that governments had created. Instead, most municipal reformers wanted the private monopolies to be regulated by the municipalities[3] or, increasingly, to become government-owned monopolies.

A by-product of that bias toward regulation and government ownership, inevitably and necessarily, would be sprawl – premature and uneconomic development at the urban periphery. Without government intervention, city development was intensive, not extensive. The early advocates of Toronto's outward expansion, frustrated as they were by the private sector's focus on profits rather than territory, understood intuitively the profit motive's role in restraining the city's expansion.

In arguing for a Greater Toronto that would unify the numerous utility systems that then existed in Toronto and its suburbs, Maclean was providing the blueprint for expansion that Toronto would broadly follow in the years to come. The settlements surrounding Toronto could not grow rapidly without expanded government control over water, sewage, and transportation systems because the local controls that then governed these systems, whether public or private, inherently constrained growth. Water systems were very costly, particularly if the water was to supply fire hydrants under great pressure.[4] To justify their expense, a dense population needed to reside in their proximity.[5] An even greater constraint presented itself in transportation, where private transit provided service along Toronto thoroughfares. To operate profitably, the transit lines required a dense population along their routes. Transit companies happily expanded service where they could earn profits; they were loath to expand where doing so would hurt their shareholders.

Maclean and other exponents of Greater Toronto championed the approach of Adam Beck, the firebrand politician who in 1906 had become the founder of the Hydro-Electric Power Commission, the continent's first major public power utility. In the same way that Beck promised to extend the electricity system into small communities by bringing it into public ownership and achieving vast economies of scale, Maclean foresaw vast public monopolies in transit and waterworks as well as power. In public hands, without the limitations inherent in private ownership, Maclean accurately foresaw, the city could grow rapidly and outward:

> Let me tell you why the city ought to have public ownership in regard to these things, especially when it is a matter of growth and development. It is that when you have public ownership you can do with your own whatever you like, whenever you like. Now when you own the Street Railway you can do with it what you like, and you can take it where you want the city to extend, and you can let it extend that way. Now we are tied up to a company within our own borders that won't let the city grow the way the citizens want it to grow. They say they will elect to give us the extensions or [rail]roads they wish, so that the extension and growth of the city today is tied up by a corporation which has tied up adjacent municipalities too. This will strangle the growth and extension of Toronto unless it is remedied ... Let us today deal with these questions from the point of view of a Greater Toronto and the fifty or one hundred square miles that we propose that Toronto should be. Let us do it on the big lines, because the big lines are the cheap lines. It is just as easy to finance a proposition for a big thing, with a sinking fund for 40 or 50 years, on a large scale, as it is on a small scale – in fact, it is better.[6]

Maclean's Greater Toronto would be a metropolis of a million people in ten to fifteen years' time, but it would not resemble the great North American cities of the day. With government intervention, he predicted, Toronto would not grow so much upwards as outwards, and its population would not suffer congestion. Toronto would be uncrowded because it would be sprawling: 'We can set out at the coming elections, we can pledge our candidates to this idea of a Greater Toronto, and we can go to the next session of the Legislature for necessary legislation. A Greater Toronto not only means a concentration of wealth, but lots of land for its people to live on. The town can be spread out.'

Maclean spoke at a time of rapid geographic growth, following a series of annexations. Toronto's area doubled in the last two decades of the nineteenth century, and it was in the midst of doubling again. But the annexations had also been sowing discontent, as the populace came to realize their cost. C.S. Clark in his 1898 book, *Of Toronto the Good: The Queen City of Canada as it Is*, described Toronto's dizzying growth:

> It was in the year 1883 that Toronto became land hungry and began to stretch forth ambitious hands to seize adjoining sections of the County of York. Bear in mind that up to this date Bloor Street on the north, Dufferin street on the west, and virtually the Don on the east marked the boundaries of our city, whose area was 6,771 acres. In 1883, Yorkville threw in its lot with the Queen City and became St. Paul's Ward. Its area was 543 acres. Its eastern boundary was Sherbourne street and its western a line just east of Bedford road. In 1884, St. Matthew's and St. Mark's ward were born, a total increase to Toronto's area of 2,346 acres. For just three years the city remained content, and then came the addition of a strip 200 feet deep on the north side of Kingston road (now Queen street), containing 57 acres, the new annex of 209 acres, 99 acres of Rosedale quickly followed in the succeeding year; 1,052 acres, including Seaton village, 91 acres between High Park and the west limit of Parkdale, and about 68 acres which carried St. Paul's hard up to the top of the hill above the C.P.R. Hemmed in by the city on three sides, Parkdale next joined fortunes with Toronto and in 1889 added St. Alban's Ward, a fair-sized debt and 650 acres of land to the municipality. This was the last accession to our area, excepting a small strip of 35 acres on the east side of Greenwood's line, which was acquired in 1890. Toronto now discovered that she had grown even too strong, and that she had acquired enough territory to hold all the citizens we are likely to have for the next 50 years. Hand in hand with this tremendous extension of territory went the local improvements and the increase of our debenture debt, and for the last six years citizens have been wondering what all the territory was ever wanted for, and have been execrating the insane speculative mania which sewered and block paved and sidewalked the grassy swards of the county of York's farm lands.[7]

The expansion, Clark lamented, had come at the city's great detriment. 'Those best qualified to speak authoritatively see in this large extension of our territory all the woes in the way of taxation which now afflict the city. Had there been added not thousands of acres of what has been fitly designated goose pastures, but, say, Parkdale and Yorkville and its suburbs, we should now have a compact city, light taxation, land valuable, and a better and more prosperous population.'

The public's resentment at the growing taxation incurred 'to illuminate cow pastures,' as one reporter put it, finally put a brake to the city's expansion. In 1911, when North Toronto tried to join the city, tax-weary Toronto residents voted down the proposal in a plebiscite. The following year, North Toronto tried again. This time it succeeded, but only because Toronto city council bypassed the public and absorbed North Toronto without a plebiscite. Forest Hill (then called Spadina Heights) was refused in 1912, and again in 1922.[8] North Toronto's would be the last amalgamation that Toronto would see in decades.

As a result of the amalgamations, taxes in Toronto soon rose by more than 50 per cent. To bring municipal services in the annexed areas to Toronto standards, the city calculated, city taxpayers paid $2 for each $1 paid by taxpayers in the annexed areas.[9] To make matters worse, Toronto became laden with debt. As the first report of the Toronto Housing Commission discovered, by the end of the First World War about one-quarter of Toronto's growing debt stemmed from 'the carrying out of local improvement works, and a large portion of these have been done in newly annexed districts.'

With the lesson of uneconomic expansion so fresh, Toronto lost its penchant for a sprawling Greater Toronto, and resolutely refused future amalgamation offers. In the 1920s many of Toronto's suburbs, gambling that they would grow quickly by providing their residents with services, overcommitted themselves. Property taxes rose rapidly, leading many residents to default on their payments. In York Township, for example, 22 per cent of taxes went unpaid in 1926, rising to 27 per cent in 1929. By the 1930s, with the Great Depression accelerating the rate of default, the precarious finances of most suburbs became untenable. When suburbs raised taxes on their remaining residents, in an attempt to make up the shortfall, still more residents defaulted. The suburbs, to escape their financial quagmire, then asked Toronto to annex them. Toronto refused, even though doing so forced most of the suburbs into bankruptcy, leading the province to assume their financial affairs.[10]

The lesson of uneconomic expansion faded by the late 1940s, however, and the lure of rationalizing services in a Greater Toronto reappeared. Planners of all political stripes decided that Toronto should incorporate the suburbs around the city, and Toronto politicians agreed.[11] But most suburban politicians strenuously opposed the merger, which would cost them their local autonomy. A compromise was struck: the local politicians would keep control over local services, such as street cleaning and garbage collection, while a metropolitan government would take responsibility for public transit, water and sewage, and other costly infrastructure. In effect, the amalgamation would occur in two stages, the first being the creation of Metropolitan Toronto. With Metro Toronto in place, the 'way is left open for eventual amalgamation of the constituent municipalities,' the new Metro chairman declared shortly after Metro's creation.[12]

The second stage of the amalgamation took place in 1998, when the City of Toronto finally obtained what it wished for at mid-century. And no sooner did the city extend itself to become the Greater Toronto that reformers envisaged at the turn of the century, than other reformers, seeking a Greater Toronto still, pressed their case for a further integration of city services with their outlying areas.

As before, the integration involved the uneconomic expansion of municipal services, without which a sprawling Greater Toronto would be impossible. As always, the sprawl would be brought to us by governments.

1 How Private Transit Hobbled Sprawl

Toronto World founder and parliamentarian W.F. Maclean, like Toronto's other influential reformers at the turn of the twentieth century, opposed the high population densities that were then the hallmark of all great cities in the world. To thwart the traditional patterns of development, and spread the population out among a much larger territory, he understood the paramountcy of nationalizing transportation systems, particularly the public transit (or traction) systems that were then run by private companies.

Few developers built housing in outlying areas that weren't served by public transit systems, and even when they did, people were reluctant to settle there because of the time and expense involved in commuting to city jobs. Maclean and other reformers wanted to minimize these obstacles to populating the outskirts by subsidizing the cost of transit routes to the countryside, so that all customers paid the same fare. With a single fare, a resident in the countryside could commute into the city for the same cost as a transit customer taking a short trip within the city, removing the natural financial disadvantage of living far from work. Without a single fare, the reformers' dream of extending the transit lines to the suburbs to create a rapidly growing Greater Toronto would be, quite literally, stopped dead in its tracks:

> Greater Toronto, to my mind, is dependent upon this more than anything else, and a proposition requiring immediate attention is the creation of this great east and west street, made up of Bloor, one of the old concession lines and a high-level viaduct over the Don. Put the street car system on that street and you are right in touch with Toronto Junction and East Toronto and you are in touch with them on your own property, and you can give

those suburbs a single fare into Toronto, and the same thing will come in regard to Yonge Street. It is a shame that East Toronto and North Toronto are at the mercy of the traction line now in the city and have to pay two fares to get into the city of which they are really citizens ... if you want to have a Greater Toronto and want to do something to make it greater, you must be absolute masters of the traction system and you ought to get legislation to allow you to recover that traction system.[1]

The legislation that Maclean demanded would expropriate the private sector system that then operated in Toronto, as well as the various suburban lines that then existed, creating one large government monopoly.

Our rights in this direction have already been provided for in the Beck law enabling us to recover the electrical franchise. Let us go further in connection with the street railways and then we will be able not only to take over the Toronto system but all the outlying systems and consolidate them with the city system so as to give the people a single fare and the control of the streets and the traction on the streets. We can give entrance to every outside radial road that cares to come into Toronto. All these will come and will help to make the city great, and will only come if you start on these right lines.

Radial roads – commuter railroads operating on diagonal roads that would connect cities to suburban developments – were all the fashion in the heady days of the early 1900s, and a standard feature in the visionary transportation plans then put forward to revamp cities. Toronto's Civic Guild of Art,[2] a voluntary organization of leading businessmen, professions, and Board of Trade members, unveiled its proposal in 1909 and in 1910, in a speech entitled 'The Evolution of a Greater Toronto,' William Houston, a *Toronto Globe* editor, proposed an electrified ring road around the built-up area, along with radial lines and road extensions into undeveloped lands. Like others, Houston saw an inevitability to Toronto's growth. He spoke of 'how greatly the city has expanded [and] the certainty that the expansion will be greater in the future than it has been in the past.' With certain growth and the government's power of expropriation, the visionary reformers believed, the sweeping changes to the city's transportation systems would occur at little or no cost:

Looking to the future, we should have a sea-wall drive at least 15 miles long from the Humber River to the Scarboro' town-line, including the

Island. We should have as its counterpart a boulevard from the mouth of the Humber, inland and around the city to the lake shore at Scarboro, at least 25 miles long, making a continuous drive, with electric car tracks of 40 miles. This would be accomplished at a comparatively small cost to the city if the property lying on each side of the boulevard were secured for the purpose of being resold at the highest price obtainable on account of the construction of the drive.[3]

The notion that suburban transit developments were all but risk-free – 'build it and they will come' was then a common sentiment – came of the success that many transit operators were experiencing south of the border. Suburban streetcars, often owned by real estate developers, commonly extended into new subdivisions before customers were present. But the boosterism was often misplaced. Many developers went bankrupt when the economy soured before they could recoup their investments, including in Canada, as Toronto developers knew all too well.

In the 1880s, private developers had created the Toronto Belt Line Corporation to speculate on land a short distance north of the city's built up area, between what is now St Clair and Eglinton avenues. To market their lots, they formed the Belt Line Railway Company, a commuter line that would be abandoned during construction because a depression had hit Toronto. The Belt Line's subsequent owners, the Grand Trunk Railway, also failed to make the transit line a paying proposition. After acquiring the Belt Line at a distressed price, it completed construction and began running trains in 1892. By 1894, its original schedule of twenty-four trips a day had been slashed to six, and then it, too, was forced to abandon the line. By the time Maclean and Houston were painting their optimistic scenarios for the future, the Belt Line's tracks were in the process of being torn up and the only commuters who used the right of way did so on foot.[4] A string of other suburban lines in the Toronto area that had experienced rocky rides also spoke to the perils of suburban transit, as did the spectacular collapse of the Montreal Park and Island Railway in 1898.[5] As transit industrialist Charles Porteous then observed:

This object lesson before the people of Canada is going to prevent them putting money into suburban roads, and make who have it there feel blue. Something like this is what I have been waiting for for some years ... There has only been one good done by this profligate building of suburban Railways, namely to put a barrier around urban properties, with plenty of danger signals both to the investor and the urban roads themselves, as to the danger of premature expansion.[6]

The Toronto reformers who touted their Greater Toronto had good reason to advocate public ownership of public transit: Toronto's private transit company, the Toronto Railway Company, baulked at the reformers' grand plans. Fearing the consequences of 'premature expansion' into sparsely populated suburbs, the company refused to risk its shareholders' capital. Neither could reformers convince other private companies to speculate on suburban services.[7]

The city was less risk-averse. It decided to enter the streetcar business by building civic transit lines to the suburbs, in areas that were partially built up. Once again, the promoter's optimism proved to be unwarranted and the civic lines, too, lost money. As a consequence, the city set aside its plans to rapidly extend service to the suburbs, leading Toronto to expand compactly, rather than to sprawl.

As put by geographer Richard Harris in his detailed history of Toronto's development in the first half of the twentieth century,

> the effect of TRC [Toronto Railway Company] policy was to encourage a relatively dense pattern of settlement. Even if suburban commuters were willing to walk across the municipal boundary to reach the end of a car ride, the caution of the TRC discouraged low-density settlement. At the end of the company's franchise, the city of Toronto had a population density of 20,200 persons per square mile, ranking second among all cities on the continent, leading New York [18,800 persons/sq. mile] and exceeded only by Jersey City [22,900 persons/sq. mile]. Such densities themselves were good for business, since they encouraged ridership, an effect that lasted well beyond the TRC's franchise into the automobile era.[8]

Toronto would grow rapidly and compactly for the balance of the decade and throughout the 1920s,[9] becoming one of the continent's most prosperous cities. Because few uneconomic lines were built to the suburbs, the development that occurred beyond the city limits also tended to be compact, within walking distance of the end of the transit line. The suburban communities that sprang up, typically modest, working-class neighbourhoods of small houses built on narrow, city-like lots, would, by the 1920s, allow for economic public transit service. The city and its outskirts, in this way, grew efficiently, with transit services provided after they could be economically justified.

As soon as Toronto's city government took over the transit system in 1921, the compact character of Toronto began to change. The Toronto Railway Company had been the most profitable transit operator of its size on the continent, almost four times as profitable as U.S. systems, which were commonly forced to provide subsidized service.[10] The city-owned Toronto Transportation Commission, which took over the responsibility of providing transit services, immediately raised its fares by 50 per cent and then applied its profits to expanding the system.[11] In the next decade the TTC more than doubled its streetcar track, accelerating the development of the suburbs and laying the ground work for the low-density development that would follow.

Yet the immediate harm done to the city would be limited. For one thing, because the suburbs had become fairly well populated by the 1920s, many of the suburban routes that the TTC built were profitable, or could be operated at a modest loss. For another, the TTC, in inheriting the Toronto Railway Company's personnel, had also inherited a culture of economic discipline. 'It had to be self-supporting. Not a penny must go out of your taxes toward the operation of the railway or towards the debt charges,' a TTC assistant general manager proudly recalled decades later.[12]

Because the TTC was entirely reliant on its passengers for its financing, it focused on attracting paying customers. This business necessity led it to resist fiercely the suburban politicians' call for a single fare. Unlike many other public systems, the TTC introduced zone fares – the longer the trip, the greater the fare – thus protecting city customers from the need to further subsidize those in the suburbs. Its relative independence also led it to become one of the continent's most successful public agencies, a model to transit operators on both sides of the border. As long as the TTC operated on a sound financial basis, transit subsidies from city customers to those in the suburbs were modest, and premature suburbanization was held largely in check.

The politicization of the TTC and its great conversion into an agent of sprawl would not occur until after 1953, with the creation of the Municipality of Metropolitan Toronto. Metro Toronto, a regional government that included the City of Toronto and its immediate suburbs, was created primarily to deliver subsidized public services to Toronto's suburbs. To reflect the Toronto Transportation Commission's new emphasis on carrying commuters from one jurisdiction to another, its name was changed to the Toronto Transit Commission. More importantly, with Metro's creation the TTC stopped acting as a self-supporting and largely independent organization.

The new TTC began with the best of intentions, determined to retain its customers in the face of competition from the automobile through fiscal prudence and high service levels. In the United States, government-regulated transit utilities were falling into disrepair, cutting back on service, becoming unreliable, and consequently losing customers. That would not happen in Toronto, the TTC's Allan Lamport insisted: 'while some people think that in some cities in the United States, transit is supposed to have slipped, I say they themselves have permitted it to slip. The Transit Commission you have today and the Metropolitan Council have certainly knuckled down to the task of safe-guarding transit and safeguarding the needs of the 60 per cent of the population who depend on public transit, and because of this I say that this area is being well served.'

Lamport was affirming the TTC's need to operate on a sound financial footing, and the impossibility of its providing the same level of service, at the same price, to low-density suburban areas:

> To illustrate how important population density is to an area, let me show you another comparison. Lower density areas are just as anxious to get transit as those in the City of Toronto. Representatives of these are Scarborough, Etobicoke, and North York, where the density is less than 4.5 persons per acre. And, to the planners of these subdivisions, again we point out that the less people you have per acre, the more vacant land our buses have to pass and to serve them with an equal fare is not possible, when you have 3.75 persons per acre in Scarborough, Etobicoke with 4.47 per acre, North York with 4.50 per acre. We cannot give the same kind of rapid transit service there and tie up the money that we can in the dense area of the City of Toronto, which runs between 60 and 73 persons per acre. Just imagine 4.50 per acre compared to 60 and 73 per acre. So you can see why there would be some complaints against us and why transportation cannot be supplied for the same fare.[13]

In fact, although the TTC advocated sound financial management, the transit subsidies to suburbanites had begun immediately upon Metro Toronto's creation. Metro took over the Toronto Transportation Commission without paying any compensation to the City of Toronto.[14] Then, much as occurred in 1921, when the TTC first took over from the private transit company, the TTC rapidly expanded transit services in the suburbs.

During the TTC's first ten years under Metro Toronto ownership, the TTC's bus route mileage increased by 75 per cent, with almost all of the expansion taking place in the suburban areas. This expansion fully doubled the annual mileage of bus services in the suburbs, to ten million miles. But unlike the expansion to the suburbs of the 1920s, which occurred at a time of immense population growth and culminated in record ridership levels by the end of the decade, the TTC's expansion following its takeover by Metro soon led to a deteriorating system and a per capita ridership that plummeted by 38 per cent in a decade.

The controversy, again, revolved around whether customers would need to pay in proportion to the distance travelled. To minimize the subsidies to the suburbs, the TTC initially brought in a five-zone fare system. Due to the pressure to serve low-density areas that Lamport would soon lament, the five zones were reduced to three in 1956 and to two in 1962. (Zones were abolished altogether in 1973.)[15]

It had taken less than a decade for the TTC to become beholden to political needs. As decried in an editorial in the *Globe and Mail* on 2 February 1962:

> The legal fiction that the Toronto Transit Commission is an autonomous body and not under the control of Metro Council is wearing thinner by the week. Only a few days ago, Metro Chairman William Allen suggested that the Council would have to subsidize extension of bus services into the suburbs which the TTC cannot or will not serve. Now the Metro Executive Committee is worrying that the Commission may not even be able to pay its agreed share of the capital cost of the east-west subway line. A joint TTC-Metro meeting will be held today to examine the financial prospects.
>
> The basis of the TTC's former autonomy was that it was able to pay its own way; the system made operating profits and was able to finance its own development. The moment this happy state of affairs came to an end, and the Commission had to call upon Metro for financial help, autonomy vanished in practice, although the legal theory remained.
>
> Metro began to pay the piper, first with fare stabilization grants and then by assuming a major share of the cost of the new subway, and Metro began to call the tune. The members of the Council felt, quite properly, that if they were going to hand over the taxpayers' money to the TTC, they wanted a voice in how it was going to be spent.
>
> It is already clear that Metro is going to have to take over an ever increasing share of the financing of transportation. The Commission has admitted that it cannot make any contribution towards the cost of the proposed Spadina subway and has indicated that it will be forced, within the next few years, to request an operating subsidy. Its chairman has also expressed the belief that a 20-cent fare will be necessary.

The TTC's uneconomic expansion, which occurred at the same time that people began owning automobiles in large numbers, led the TTC to cut back services in the city as cost-saving measures. The TTC's quandary, as a TTC Commissioner told a Metro executive committee at the time, was between cutting services or raising fares. As paraphrased by the Toronto *Star*, 'in either case, [we would be] chasing passengers off the system, and reducing its usefulness to the Metro area.'[16] The Toronto Transit Commission in 1967 acknowledged that 'most of the routes in the outlying Metro districts lose money for several years and must be supported by the rest of the system.[17] By the 1970s, after the single fare was introduced, the system of overcharging city users to support suburbanites amounted to a subsidy of $110 a year per suburban transit commuter.[18]

Some of the TTC's most uneconomic expansions involved its subway system. Prior to Metro's formation, the TTC had embarked on an ambitious subway-building program, all of it financed from its own operations, along congested streets whose heavy traffic justified the investment.[19] The first of these, a 4.5-mile stretch along Yonge Street from Union Station to Eglinton Avenue, financed with a $25 million surplus that the TTC had accumulated during the war years, was almost complete by the time Metropolitan Toronto government assumed office in January 1954.

Future subway developments would not be self-financing, nor would they exclusively serve high-density routes. In the 1960s, Metro extended the subway system east into Scarborough and west into Etobicoke, through areas that were not then, and remain today, too low in population density to justify subway service.[20] It built the Spadina line north through thinly populated suburban areas. These expansions, determined solely by political determinations and wholly unrelated to financial viability, would set the stage for the immense budget deficits that became a permanent feature of the transit system.

Before Metro degraded the economics of transit service, the TTC was a going concern, generating the profits needed to maintain the existing system and to expand the system by investing in subways and surface routes. All city lines made money. After the system became fully politicized, it became unable to pay its own way, first for new expansions, then for its own maintenance. Service suffered, rates rose, ridership fell, and new subway routes were shelved. Today, virtually all routes, whether in the city or the newly absorbed suburbs, lose money.

2 Living at Close Quarters

At the turn of the nineteenth century, the population of Canada's major cities was exploding, with Toronto especially emerging as a new metropolis. In 1876, its population was 68,000; a mere quarter century later, in 1901, it had tripled to 208,000, and had reached 522,000 by 1921.

These astounding rates of growth, sustained over decades, had never before been seen in Canada. Because the population increase was unprecedented, the government initially had few rules in place to control the development that accompanied it. Toronto grew organically, with scant commercial and residential zoning regulations, and few restrictions on the uses to which buildings and lots could be put. With such decisions made by individual households or by developers, diversity flowered. Different ethnic groups chose different neighbourhoods, different types of occupations, different types of investments, and different routes to prosperity. But whether the groups settled within Toronto or in its many residential or industrial suburbs, one characteristic did not differ: most people chose to live in close proximity to others to best further their goals.

The population growth in the first decades of the twentieth century came mostly from immigration. By 1931, when Toronto's population reached 631,000, immigrants represented almost 40 per cent of the city's population, giving it the highest proportion on the continent.[1] Most immigrants to Canada had come from the largely urbanized British Isles. The unskilled among the British immigrants became farm labourers while the skilled – typically mechanics, metal workers, and other tradesmen – eased the shortages present in Toronto and other cities. Dr Peter H. Bryce, chief medical officer of the Department of the Interior in Ottawa, described for a Toronto audience how these and other immigrants settled:

The British who were not artisans have been sent to the farmers of the country, the artisans have been found work here and in many other places, and the community is constantly crying out for more help. The Italian has almost wholly gone out on to railway work. We have then left 2,000 Hebrews, and some of these have gone into the Temiskaming district and begun settlements there. The balance have, we assume, remained in this or other cities.

That the British follow their instincts, the peculiar instincts of the Teuton, whatever country he has lived in or been brought to, is shown in the fact that in the suburbs and in the outlying parts of the city, we have hundreds and thousands of houses, first shacks, put up two or three years ago, which have now become good houses, filled with British-thinking, British-speaking, British-acting citizens.[2]

The suburban homes of the self-sufficient communities that Bryce was referring to were mostly built on unserviced lots just outside the city limits, to escape the city's high property taxes[3] while enjoying proximity to the city. They also escaped the city regulations that had begun to raise building costs and squeeze out the poor. '[There are no] restrictions as to building,' the developer of one working-class district advertised; 'the building restrictions are very moderate,' another assured. 'No matter how simple the first structure of your home may be, in a few years all settlers will have enlarged and beautified their dwellings.'[4]

This 'shacktown fringe,' as a *Toronto Globe* writer called it, was typically located within walking distance of a streetcar line, and built to high densities. 'Shackland's dwellings extend around Toronto,' an author wrote in 'Visit to Shackland in Toronto's suburbs' in 1907. 'There is scarcely a terminating car in the city but taps [them].' Wilfrid Dinnick, a philanthropist and founder of Lawrence Park Estates, wrote of the dense development that the British created: 'Always first in the opening up of new districts, the most recent British population is buying further from the built-up outlying districts of the city than has been customary ... Every year districts settled by British emigrants are being sold by them as the district becomes thickly populated and the land more valuable ... many of them keep moving [further out] as the city advances.'

To meet the demand for housing, the outlying townships permitted rural properties to be subdivided into small lots, making these suburbs attractive to developers and self-builders alike. On Coxwell Avenue on the city's fringe, a 1912 photo from the City Archives shows three modest ten- to twelve-foot-wide houses tightly built next to each other on lots separated by two-foot-wide lanes, the pattern repeated in other series of houses visible in the background to the photo. 'By buying small lots and using their own labour to erect what began as very modest structures, even unskilled workers who worked downtown could afford to settle at the urban fringe,' concluded geographer Richard Harris in *Unplanned Suburbs*, a study of Toronto in the first half of the twentieth century.[5] The shacktowns were modest but 'passable as a makeshift,' economist James Mavor of University of Toronto stated in 1923, referring to the pre-WWI shacktowns. Engineer W.A. McLean that same year stated that 'the history of "shack-towns" as a rule is that they develop into districts of comfortable homes for labouring men.' Group of Seven legend Lawren Harris called shacktowns picturesque, and painted them respectfully.

Suburban residents weren't all commuters, however. In the industrial suburbs, which sprang up partly to accommodate industries that were abandoning small towns, workers would both live and work in close proximity, to save commuting time and the cost of public transit. A study of the Heintzman piano factory in the industrial suburb of West Toronto Junction (better known today as 'The Junction') found that almost all its workers in the late 1880s could easily walk to work.

In contrast to the 'good houses' that British immigrants, step-by-step, built for themselves on vacant lots just outside the city, other immigrants – chiefly Jews and Italians – moved into existing housing in the heart of the city, in the slums of St John's Ward.[6] The Ward, population 10,000 in 1907, was more a shantytown than a tenement slum: It was a collection of streets and laneways, full of run-down single-family dwellings. As with earlier waves of immigrants, the newcomers rented space there to be within easy walking distance of the factories along Spadina Avenue and other industrial streets. Bryce, a medical doctor, deplored their living conditions, including 'the absence of new houses in the congested district, the readiness with which the landlord can put in two where there was previously one, the tendency which there is among a certain class of landlords to do as they say in the Chicago Report, and similarly in the New York Report of 1894; "that they will fill up all their space, and build up their houses to Heaven, if they were allowed to do so, in order to lessen the amount of assessment, and the amount of ground rent."'[7]

Notwithstanding the landlords' efforts to keep their costs down by expanding the rentable space, rents had almost doubled in the decade to 1907, when Bryce delivered his comments. A major reason for Toronto's housing inflation prior to the First World War, a federal Board of Inquiry into the Cost of Living in Canadian cities would later determine, was the city's 'more severe Housing By-law restrictions,' chiefly a draconian 1904 bylaw that outlawed wood-frame buildings throughout the city.[8] The federal Department of Labour's *Labour Gazette* reported in 1905 that 'the stringency of the building regulations is stated to be a deterrent to erecting cheap houses in the city.' It explained that 'many working men are building small houses for themselves beyond the city limits, to escape the stringent regulations forbidding the erection of frame buildings in the city.'

Toronto's regulations not only spurred suburban building, they also forced the city's poor into the relatively low-cost slums. Though far from ideal, the resulting system of slum rental housing nevertheless functioned well, Bryce asserted.

> We have absorbed, perfectly I think, the thousand Italians and some three thousand Jews, who were in Toronto, according to the Census of 1901. We must have added in each year since a definite number. This year, I pointed out, we have had 1,900 Hebrews come in, and some 4,000 Italians and 6,000 others, largely Hungarians and Poles; so that we must have some of them here, and they have overflowed into St. John's ward and other parts of the city.'[9]

History would affirm Bryce's judgment. The non-British immigrants in the slums would prosper and come to live in their own homes. The factory workers among them typically started by finding inexpensive housing in the Ward, or they might board with one of the many working-class families that took in boarders to finance their own homes. Later, after the boarders had accumulated savings of their own, they would apply it to a down payment for a home for themselves, and likewise take in boarders to help pay the mortgage. Jews, for example, often bought large homes, converted them to lodging houses, and let individual rooms out to more recent Jewish arrivals.[10] Within a decade, the Jewish lodgers would often have their own homes, and be taking in their own lodgers.[11] The Jewish ownership rate of 4 per cent in 1901 became 36 per cent by 1915 and by the 1920s the more affluent Jews began to settle nearby Forest Hill, helping to make it Toronto's most affluent suburb.

The immigrants who worked in retail, as opposed to those who worked in the factories, might put their savings into the purchase of a store, and live in an apartment above it. By 1912, Italians owned more than half of Toronto's fruit stores and were also prominent as barbers, innkeepers, and music teachers, earning above average incomes and status.[12] Other ethnic groups found different niches, and also acquired for themselves incomes unattainable to them in their countries of origin. In such ways, lower-income immigrant families would develop large portions of Toronto, and home ownership rates among blue-collar workers approached that of white-collar workers and professionals. By 1921, according to the census, fully 60 per cent of Torontonians lived in their own homes, up from an also impressive 27 per cent in 1899 and by far the highest of any major city in the continent.[13]

The city grew like topsy, but the growth resembled anything but sprawl. In 1901, 95 per cent of the combined population of the city and its suburbs lay in the city, compared to 76 per cent for the twenty largest cities in the United States. In 1911, the proportion remained high, at 92 per cent, as in 1921, when it was 85 per cent. Not only did Toronto have the highest population density of any large city in the continent,[14] its suburbs were also relatively dense, as were the districts along the streetcar routes from city to suburb. The routes themselves were densely developed, chock-a-block with shops topped by apartments.

In some cases, dense districts were curtailed. Following pressure from property owners in the then-affluent Moss Park Place area[15] who feared that a proposed bakery would harm their property values, the city in 1904 obtained from the province the right to control 'the location, erection, and use of buildings for laundries, butcher shops, stores, and manufactories.' By 1905, the city applied this law broadly to entire neighbourhoods, after petitions from affluent Annex and South Rosedale residents, although no one had yet proposed controversial business developments there. But most of the city, and in particular the industrial and working-class districts, were exempt from these restrictions, giving the poor the chance to prosper. In this relatively tolerant environment, Toronto and its suburbs grew rapidly and pragmatically, thanks to a citizenry that looked after its own housing, however imperfectly. 'Subdivided park or farm lots were developed unevenly, without any overall plan, but this approach provided affordable homes for many working-class families,' a government study of that period would later conclude.[16]

Homes were mostly built by developers, often in a string along the same street or in subdivisions. Some developers, not content with putting one house upon an urban lot, shoe-horned two or more per lot, and deeded parts of lots to homeowners as they saw fit. More significantly, the relative absence of building standards enabled individual homeowners to contribute greatly to the housing stock by wielding their own hammers.[17]

'The Most Convenient Place for the Workingman to Build His Home,' boasted a 1912 ad that appeared in the Toronto *Evening Telegram*, selling lots in the Silverthorn Park Addition on St Clair Avenue West, a working-class district in what was then the northwest part of the city. 'The building restrictions are very moderate,' it assured. For those who wanted less guesswork and more guidance in the building of their houses, companies such as Sears sold home kits that offered a variety of house plans. These mail-order homes came complete with directions, nails and fixtures, allowing entire houses to be assembled on site, often for less than $2,000. Many of the 'four-square' style homes common in fashionable Toronto neighbourhoods such as High Park and the Annex were built this way.[18] All told, a large segment of city housing built between 1900 and 1913 was self-built, with estimates varying from 25 per cent to 40 per cent.[19]

Toronto's era of relative laissez-faire in housing led to innovation and much of its finest housing stock. It was in this period of rapid, apparently haphazard growth that the semi-detached homes so prevalent in Toronto – affordable because they required less land to build and less fuel to heat – became a norm. This period also produced Toronto's historic districts, ones that conservationists would come to prize and individuals would later gentrify. Most of all, this period created abundant, affordable housing. In 1930 the Toronto Chamber of Commerce placed a sign over the Humber Bridge that announced: 'Welcome to Toronto, City of Homes.' Toronto by then had been so characterized for decades, due to the resourcefulness of its developers and its citizens in generating single-family dwellings.

3 Toronto the Good

Toronto, the City of Homes, was more than a city of single-family houses. During the first few decades of the twentieth century, Toronto would also become a city of low-rise apartment buildings. Toronto's first apartment building, the St George Mansions, completed in 1903, and its second, the Alexandria,[1] completed the following year, provided prestigious addresses for visiting professionals and businessmen as well as Toronto's elite: doctors, lawyers, judges, professors, bank managers, and company directors were among their tenants.[2] More modest apartment buildings sprang up, too, to appeal to a growing market of residents attracted to a modern, metropolitan lifestyle, and who didn't want the expense and commitment of time needed to maintain a house and yard.[3] By 1913, Toronto had 113 apartment buildings, compared to four in 1905.[4]

After the First World War, the rate of apartment building increased to meet the housing needs of large numbers of returning servicemen, but by 1921, apartments still represented just 4 per cent of all dwelling units. The apartment boom then began in earnest, and became unstoppable until the stock market crash of 1929 and the Great Depression that followed. By 1931, the city's apartment builders had created more than 20,000 units, typically in three- and four-storey walk-ups. These often handsome buildings housed perhaps one-tenth of Toronto's population. Apartment buildings were also built in clusters just outside the city's limits, in upscale Forest Hill and in York Township.[5]

The widespread popularity of apartment buildings was all the more remarkable in light of the intense opposition that they attracted from many segments of society. One source of opposition came from immediate neighbours in single-family homes. They saw apartment buildings, even luxury ones, as a threat to their property values, and lobbied government to have them stopped. In 1905, after apartment building developers purchased a lot at the northeast corner of Spadina Road and Lowther Avenue in Toronto's fashionable Annex district, a group of neighbours protested to the city's Board of Control; ultimately, the neighbours purchased the lot from the developers at a premium to prevent the development. The developers then proceeded to build an apartment building at the southeast corner of the same intersection, leading to the city's first attempt at regulating apartment buildings – it required the building to be set back 25 feet from the property line, a provision that would have stopped the project had the courts not overturned it.[6]

Real estate agents, fearing loss of commissions, were also alarmed by the popularity of apartment buildings. In 1912 a deputation of agents requested that city council limit 'the erection of new buildings or the conversion of existing dwellings for anything other than a dwelling house for one family.'[7] While financial self-interest motivated opposition from immediate neighbours and real estate agents, a more general opposition arose from those who considered apartment buildings a dangerous social innovation that compromised child-rearing, promoted sexual promiscuity, and otherwise threatened family life.[8] Apartment buildings were not only popular with business travellers but also with new immigrants, young childless couples, and the many single women who, after leaving the farm for jobs in the big city, lived two or three to an apartment unit. An article in Toronto's *Canadian Architect and Builder* in 1903 associated the convenience of apartments with indifference to family life: 'The woman who is most envied is she who has the least care. Not only is pride in their families vanishing but pride in their housekeeping as well ... apartment life will complete the process.' Toronto's *Globe* warned that apartment buildings would produce 'stunted children and unhappy adults [hurting the city's] morals and its health.'

Toronto, in fact, was preoccupied with public morality. In the great migration from the farm to Toronto that occurred in the late nineteenth and early twentieth centuries, the majority of migrants were single women. In 1851 the ratio of women to men in Toronto was almost even: 102.7 females to 100 males. By 1901 the ratio had become 112.5 to 100. The change in ratio of single residents was even more dramatic, from 105.4 single women to 100 single men in 1881 to 120.9 to 100 in 1901. Women were abandoning the farm 'through necessity that they may live, others that they may help their parents, while no inconsiderable number are daughters of country farmers who prefer city life and fixed hours of work, even at low wages, rather than remain at home, on the farm,' reported the Ontario Bureau of Industry, a government agency that investigated the phenomenon of the working women.

Toronto the Good, as the city was then known, along with its Morality Department, the Board of Social and Moral Reform of the Presbyterian Church, the Temperance, Prohibition and Moral Reform Department of the Methodist Church of Canada, the Social Service Congress of Canada, and the Moral and Social Reform Council of Canada, among others, became obsessed with the danger to these young ladies' morals. Great pressure was placed on the female migrants to live with family members or to become live-in domestics, where they were thought to be less subject to temptation, and reproach followed those who chose to live on their own, or with other single women. The federal government's Royal Commission on the Relations of Labour and Capital inquired into why young women were increasingly choosing jobs in factories or in retail over domestic positions. The commissioners 'hounded witnesses for the vital question: Why did increasing numbers of women prefer industrial over domestic work?' wrote University of Toronto criminologist Carolyn Strange in *Toronto's Girl Problem*, her history of morality in Toronto a century ago. Employers of single women, such as Miss Burnett, a milliner who testified before the commission, provided answers such as this: 'They like to have their evenings to themselves. I suppose that is the real reason.'

Suspecting that women were driven into their disreputable conduct by deep disturbances, the Toronto General Hospital's Dr C.K. Clarke established its first outpatient psychiatric department in the heavily populated Ward in 1909. As *Toronto's Girl Problem* describes, it had as its primary purpose the collection of data on the links between feeble-mindedness, illicit sexuality, and venereal disease.

> Both male and female patients were analyzed, but the young women merited extra attention ... Clarke summarized over a decade of his work in 'A Study of 5,600 Cases Passing Through the Psychiatric Clinic.' Every one of the cases he cited in detail involved working girls whose scores on intelligence tests and confessions of illicit sexual activity provided him with the psychological evidence he sought. Sure enough, each of the women who had acquired venereal diseases or who shamelessly recounted their sexual adventures to interviewers was categorized as mentally subnormal. Those who passed the intelligence tests could still be categorized as 'high grade morons' if they failed 'to recognize the most obvious moral obligations.'

Not surprisingly, none of the women who came to the clinic was deemed to be normal. Moreover, psychiatric and medical experts were apparently the only diagnosticians qualified to spot the subnormal. They issued repeated warnings that 'morons' were dangerous precisely because they were notoriously adept at masking their subnormality until it was too late.[9]

To reformers who saw dangers to the public health in terms of moral conduct, public health concerned venereal disease, the drinking of alcohol, and, especially, the changing role of women, with its unknown consequences on society at large.[10] Throughout the industrializing world at the turn of the century, the birth rate was plummeting, and North America, where one-third of working women in large cities were either lodgers or boarders, was no exception. In Canada, women bore 189 children per 1,000 adult females in 1871 but only 94 in 1931. In Ontario during that period, the rate dropped even more, from 191 to 79. Canadian-born women, by abandoning the traditional single-family home, were abandoning their responsibilities to society, many felt, resulting in a race weakened through depopulation and feeble-mindedness. Immigrant races, thought to be less nurturing of children and more sexually wanton, would then overrun the country's more civilized British people. The consequences of novel living arrangements could not have been presented more starkly.

Apartment buildings not only faced hurdles as corruptors of public morality, they also bore the stigma of tenement houses. In a 1907 speech, Dr Peter H. Bryce, chief medical Officer of the Department of the Interior in Ottawa, warned Torontonians of the immorality that came of the crowded conditions of tenements in other cities, and the need to ensure Toronto avoided their problems:

> There is the other point – the necessity for having something added to the building by-law making it absolutely clear, that on a particular area of ground in a particular size of house, not more than so many persons can sleep. We won't talk about living in the day-time, but 'cannot sleep,' that is the point, and the only point at which we can regulate in any degree the tenement house problem. All of you see the point; for instance, in a double decker in Chicago, the Committee tells us that 127 persons lived in 70 rooms, and in one case six children and three grownup persons lived in three interior rooms, which received no outside light at all, and this was in

a new building. If that is the case there, then, our municipal health by-law or building bylaw must be amended, and in addition to that you must follow up legislation with constant inspection, because the landlord, in many cases, will simply go on to the limit ...

If we are to forget everything except the purely individual and material interests of ourselves, we are not even good political philosophers in leaving out the question of good morals, because everyone sees very well – that if our City became like New York or Chicago, in its police force, in a general disregard for law and order, that everyone's property would be affected, to put it on the lowest basis. We would be affected in every way, and we cannot separate ourselves from our neighbours, be they rich or poor.[11]

Crowded districts were deplored but less as symptoms of poverty than as creators of deviants that reveled in licentiousness and other disreputable conduct,[12] leading to sloth and poverty, lack of hygiene and disease. Dr Charles Hastings, Toronto's medical officer of health, was one of the most passionate exponents of theories conflating public health and morality.[13] He argued that the presence of 'rear houses' (built in backyards or lanes) and outhouses and the absence of indoor plumbing – an absence that was then the norm – constituted 'a danger to public morals, and in fact, an offence against public decency,' and that 'criminals and moral lepers are born in the atmosphere of physical and moral rottenness pervading the slums of large cities.' Citing Hastings, religious organizations such as the Methodist Department of Evangelism and Social Services campaigned to eradicate the overcrowded dwellings that were 'hotbeds for germination and dissemination of disease, vice, and crime.'[14] Joining them were anti-immigrant groups, alcohol prohibitionists, social workers, doctors, eugenicists, and others in the 'social purity movement,' a network determined to improve Canadian society, and especially the urban working class. These reformers seized upon public health laws, and these laws' ability to control where and how people lived, as an instrument in shaping the society they espoused. As York University sociologist Mariana Valverde described the movement in *The Age of Light, Soap, and Water*, it was an 'ambitious project to transform Canadian society.'[15]

Under pressure from reformers fearing the 'evils of tenements,' Toronto in 1912 passed a bylaw prohibiting the construction of small apartment buildings – defined as three or more units – in residential neighbourhoods. These low-rises were as a result confined to the downtown area and along the main traffic arteries already dominated by commercial buildings. The demand for apartments could not be dampened, however, frustrating the reformers, particularly since the city subsequently exempted some builders from the bylaw, or defined apartment buildings as something else – typically as 'ladies residences.'[16]

These restrictions were too lax for Hastings; he opposed all apartment dwellings. In New York City and elsewhere, housing reforms had led to the construction of 'model tenements' – apartment buildings that provided larger living quarters with bathing facilities, and large courtyards to allow air and light. Hastings mockingly equated the model tenement to a 'model boil or model toothache' and warned of a 'race suicide' if young couples lived in apartments rather than houses. Touting the value during war of being able to grow food in vegetable gardens, Hastings argued that 'probably one of the most valuable lessons learned during the past two or three years has been the value of cultivation of back yards and vacant lots,' concluding that 'It is important that we do not strangle this by tenement house or small apartment house dwellings.' To Hastings, only one form of housing met his standard: 'if we are to develop along judicial lines we must make Toronto a city of individual homes.'

Hastings' opposition to apartment buildings stemmed from a more general opposition to multi-family dwellings of all kinds. These included lodging houses, which had long been fixtures in Toronto. At the bottom end of the market were 10-cent lodging houses that provided dormitory-style beds for the near destitute. But many lodging houses enjoyed great respectability. Toronto's archives provide details of such an establishment, Mrs Agnew's Boarding House on Jarvis Street. Catherine Agnew, a middle-class widow who had been married to a physician, bought the semi-detached house around 1875. She taught at Winchester School in nearby Cabbagetown and in 1886, she lived in the house with her two children, Robert, a bank clerk, and John, a law student, as well as nine boarders.

Even such lodging houses, the reformers believed, were undesirable because they failed to provide the privacy that family life required. Without this privacy, sexual relations abound, women become debased, and girls become lured into prostitution.[17] Also for reasons of privacy, the reformers objected to families that doubled up in the same house – all constituted the 'lodger evil' that they deplored. Hastings held that 'family living conditions should be subjected to the closest scrutiny, and every effort made first to inculcate the elementary principles of sanitation and the privacy requisite to home life.' To realize his wish, Hastings decided to regulate undesirable lifestyle forms out of existence. In 1911 he convinced the city to double his budget to further his ends, and in subsequent years he won additional increases. At his request, in 1914 Toronto passed a bylaw giving its health department the right to inspect any home in the city. Inspectors then proceeded to require owners to upgrade any sanitary facilities found wanting. Because of the expense involved – an indoor toilet and wash basin could cost as much as a small house[18] – many were forced to abandon their city dwellings, even during the First World War, a time of housing shortages. Between 1913 and 1918, Toronto demolished 1,600 houses that didn't meet Hastings's standards, and otherwise stopped lodgers and second families from sharing the same premises: 'On account of the activities of the Department, coupled with improved economic conditions, most of these extra families moved out,' he would report in 1918, at the close of the war. Those forced out were disproportionately poor. Lamented a workers' paper at the time: 'You are doing an absolutely unjustifiable thing in forcing workingmen who have built little homes on streets where there are no water services, [to] install up-to-date plumbing or get out within 30 days.'[19]

Also in 1918, the Toronto Housing Commission was created, with Hastings a commissioner. It, too, deplored multi-family residences. Lamenting the decline of home ownership that occurred during the war, it stated: 'This is obviously an undesirable tendency, since the future greatness, stability, and welfare of any City depend upon the number of its inhabitants who own their own residences.' The commission promoted detached houses for their 'greater privacy – a feature which appeals very strongly to Canadians, with their marked individualism.' In the following year, the Ontario Housing Committee also took up the theme of privacy in condemning the growing practice of taking in lodgers. Family life becomes degraded when families double up, the committee stated: 'There necessarily follows a lowering of self respect and a loss of sturdy independence, factors that are essential to sound moral fibre.' The committee favoured private houses, with yards. 'If the child cannot step outside the door of his flat without being on the property of others, or cannot play out of doors except on the street or in the lane, proper moral and physical development is hardly possible. Tremendous values lie behind the term "our house."' The committee, which was charged with producing guidelines for local agencies, even discouraged the construction of large single-family homes, on the grounds that surplus rooms might be put to use for lodgers. 'If more than six rooms are provided the tendency is to make up the additional expense by subletting to roomers, usually with injurious effect to home life.'

Reformers used housing laws rigorously in promoting their morality, and they were also rigorous in the absence of laws. In 1921 the housing commission discovered that people to whom it had sold its model homes were allowing others to live under the same roof. Although the homes were now privately owned, and the commissioners no longer had jurisdiction, they nevertheless decided that 'purchasers who were subletting part, or all, of their homes be notified that they must discontinue this practise.' To further discourage unwanted forms of housing, the *Municipal Act* was amended in 1921 to permit the establishment of 'residence-only' streets. 'Residence-only' bylaws then prohibited all forms of construction other than private detached residences in areas deemed needy of protection.[20]

The success that the reformers had in discouraging lodgers and doubling up was isolated, however. As reported by the Census of Canada, the percentage of Toronto households containing more than one family rose from 4.9 per cent in 1901 to 9.2 per cent in 1911 to 10.2 per cent in 1921. In 1931, when the census recorded lodgers and doubling up separately, 23.2 per cent of households had one or more lodgers, and 31.6 per cent had either lodgers or more than one family or both. The economic logic of sharing homes, and of building new homes compactly, was thwarting the reformers and their government agencies. That left the government agencies little choice but to provide the needed housing themselves.

4 Model People, Model Suburbs

At the beginning of the twentieth century, Toronto's urban reformers were calling for curbs on unplanned housing developments. Invariably, they advocated slum clearances to eradicate the moral rot that they saw, and model housing to inculcate family values. As was the fashion in that period on both sides of the Atlantic, reformers urged the building of 'garden suburbs.'[1]

The Garden City movement had begun in the United Kingdom, where a century earlier the Industrial Revolution had left much of the countryside a shambles. With people abandoning the rural areas for higher wages, shorter work days, and entertainment in the city, many rural areas had become depopulated and economically depressed. Unable to maintain their homes, the remnants of the poverty-stricken rural population crowded into dilapidated dwellings. Water and air was polluted in the countryside, diseases rampant, life spans short.

The landmark Chadwick Report of 1842 summarized the grim lot of workers: 'That the various forms of epidemic, endemic, and other disease caused, or aggravated, or propagated chiefly amongst the labouring classes by atmospheric impurities produced by decomposing animal and vegetable substances, by damp and filth, and close and overcrowded dwellings prevail amongst the population in every part of the kingdom, whether dwelling in separate houses, in rural villages, in small towns, in the larger towns – as they have been found to prevail in the lowest districts of the metropolis.'

Public health in the working class sections of cities was no better than in the country, despite the workers' relative affluence: 'The high prosperity in respect to employment and wages, and various and abundant food, have afforded to the labouring classes no exemptions from attacks of epidemic disease, which have been as frequent and as fatal in periods of commercial and manufacturing prosperity as in any others.'[2]

Chadwick's warning motivated British society to act, but as much to protect public morality as public health. He warned that 'these adverse circumstances tend to produce an adult population short-lived, improvident, reckless, and intemperate, and with habitual avidity for sensual gratifications; that these habits lead to the abandonment of all the conveniences and decencies of life, and especially lead to the overcrowding of their homes, which is destructive to the morality as well as the health of large classes of both sexes; that defective town cleansing fosters habits of the most abject degradation and tends to the demoralization of large numbers of human beings, who subsist by means of what they find amidst the noxious filth accumulated in neglected streets and bye-places.'

The British reformers initially attempted to aid the countryside, where profound poverty compounded the miserable public health. They proposed utopian rural settlements, and inspired various industrialists and philanthropists to establish utopian villages to further the lot of rural workers and their families.[3] The culmination of nineteenth-century reform thinking came with Ebenezer Howard and his Garden City concept, an updated utopia that simultaneously sought to improve both city and rural areas. 'My proposal is that there should be an earnest attempt made to organize a migratory movement of population from our overcrowded centres to sparsely-settled rural districts,' he wrote in 1902 in *Garden Cities of To-morrow*. 'By so laying out a Garden City that, as it grows, the free gifts of Nature – fresh air, sunlight, breathing room and playing room – shall be still retained in all needed abundance.' Howard's theories soon pervaded North America, where numerous reformers were alarmed at the sweeping changes in society that came of a rapidly expanding population. In 1907 Toronto's first Housing Commission began the government's long history of promoting suburban growth as the answer to overcrowding.

City reformers wanted ideal suburban communities of single family homes, not the apartment buildings and rooming-houses that were springing up in the city, not the helter-skelter developments that were growing on the urban fringe. To control the unregulated subdividing of properties that was occurring in the suburbs – much of it by individuals building their own homes – Toronto petitioned the province for regional planning legislation, and obtained it in 1912 in the form of the *Cities and Suburbs Plans Act*, which required public approval of new subdivisions within five miles of a city.[4] Toronto City Council then instructed the surveyor's office to prepare 'a topographical survey of the suburbs in order to lay out definite roads and diagonal streets'[5] along lines it favoured. The reformers' opposition to unplanned housing developments also found favour among real estate developers, who recognized that government planning would benefit them by creating standards that discouraged self-built homes.

The federal government, too, joined the chorus for reform, and in many ways led it. Its Commission of Conservation, created in 1909 with a mandate to protect the natural environment, soon created a public health committee that promoted municipal planning to improve the lot of the poor. In 1914 it hired a giant in the field of planning, Garden City proponent Thomas Adams, to draft model town planning legislation and lobby provinces to allow their municipalities to regulate land use.[6] This task became especially consequential as the First World War progressed, and the federal government began to plan for the return of its overseas soldiers. Adams recognized that 'the problem of providing for the returning soldiers, and for the anticipated increase in immigration, would seem to provide the opportunity for making an experiment in linking up the amenities and facilities of town life with the healthy conditions of the country.'

> If, with the return of peace, there is to be a great demand for land, we need to have, not only the supply to meet that demand, but the right conditions to organize and distribute the supply. This is a problem closely connected with town development and is not remote from town planning; it is also a problem which involves a certain amount of replanning of the agricultural areas themselves. Many people, including those accustomed to living in rural districts all their lives, crave the social attractions of the towns. A factor which makes people, habituated to rural conditions, migrate to the towns will be present in a stronger degree, in connection with attempts to settle men, who, like returning soldiers, have enjoyed the intercourse and facilities of town life. Such men are not likely to take kindly to living on isolated farms in districts remote from populated centres.[7]

To make rural life palatable and profitable – 'unless we can make farming pay we cannot solve the problem of rural depression,' he believed – Adams argued for 'the provision of capital, the training of inexperienced men, the selection of suitable areas, and the proper planning of agricultural colonies.'

It is the latter with which we are concerned, and it is not the least important of the matters requiring public attention. In properly organized agricultural colonies, such as those which exist in Belgium and Holland, it is essential to have indoor rural industries situated in the village centres, and such industries could provide employment for many unsuited or unwilling to take up agricultural work. The establishment of rural industries in Canada might very well receive encouragement, apart from the question of providing for returned soldiers, with a view to increasing the number of small towns in agricultural districts and lessening the congestion of the larger cities ...

Decentralization of our manufacturing industries is as desirable in the interests of the healthy town as it is in the interests of agriculture. Canada should encourage new settlers to migrate to the small villages and towns, rather than, as in the past, to provide attractions for them to congregate in large cities. The more widespread the population is the more healthy it will be, and the more it will help to solve many problems which have been created by our having thinly scattered agricultural population on the one hand and overcrowded cities on the other.[8]

Echoing the moral concerns of the day, Adams believed these agricultural colonies would also improve the character of Canadians: 'Indoor rural industries develop individual skill, taste and character,' he declared.

The Commission of Conservation was an equally harsh critic of unplanned urban developments, as its medical advisor, Dr C.A. Hodgetts, made clear: 'Largely owing to increased immigration, the development of towns has been chaotic, and tens of thousands of so-called houses have been thrown together, which must, sooner or later, be condemned for sanitary reasons. As for town planning, there has been none. The speculative owner of property has, with the aid of the provincial land surveyor, mapped out streets and lots so as to make the most for the owners, while no thought or heed has been given to the question of how the work should be done in the best interests of the health or convenience of the community.'[9] The answer, Hodgetts believed, was to forgo profit and build cities along rational lines, which involved banning tall buildings, leaving plenty of space for thoroughfares, segregating different city functions by area,[10] and reserving thirty to fifty years of land for the city's future growth.

'It is from the standpoint of the health of the people that the all-important question of housing must be approached. Housing conditions should be regulated and supervised in a strong and almost imperative manner by a central national health authority. By such means much may be done towards conserving the nation's most valuable asset.'[11]

The reformers believed that, left to the voluntary workings of the marketplace, landlords would provide ever-smaller quarters for ever-larger numbers of people, homeowners would take in lodgers to help pay the mortgage, and overcrowding would result. The upshot would be the ruined health and public morals of the participants, to the ultimate ruin of society. Underlying the moral arguments was a belief that a more tidy and orderly system of development would be economic, in that it would overcome irrational housing decisions by rich and poor alike: 'One of the great difficulties met with everywhere in respect of the housing of the poorer people is the fact that they cluster around our city centres where land is dear, while the wealthy live on cheap land,' stated a report to the Commission of Conservation. 'To house this class properly in the outskirts should be one of the aims of town planning. This consideration leads up to the equally important one of cheap and rapid transportation for them to and from their work, as well as from one part of the town to the other.'[12] Adams, too, believed that the initial expense of the subsidies required to restructure society along rational lines would ultimately prove economic, if regulators had the absolute regulatory power needed to perform the job.

Adams proposed sweeping legislation to empower local boards 'to approve all new development and to require plans and particulars of all subdivisions and laying out of streets'[13] and to enable his vision to be realized, he travelled the country, lobbying provincial legislatures, drafting legislation, and meeting with immense success. More than any other individual, Adams legitimized the notion that Canadian governments should dictate settlement patterns; more than any individual, Adams persuaded governments that high-density living brought with it social and economic ills, and that sound policy called for the resettlement of city folk.

The reformers' answer to the overcrowded conditions of the city not only involved subsidizing rural industries to pull people away from cities; it also involved demolishing slums to push people out. They would then create model, low-density housing on the former slum site.

Toronto Co-Partnership Garden Suburbs Ltd, later renamed the Toronto Housing Company, was created to promote this approach by building low-cost publicly assisted housing.[14] Soon after its creation in 1912, it purchased two sites in the city, one suburban site in the Junction,

36 Toronto Sprawls

and a large suburban tract northeast of Toronto. Its dream of creating garden suburbs soon faded, however, as the economics of suburban development hit home: even with government subsidies, the Toronto Housing Company came to realize, suburban properties would be too poorly served by transit to attract tenants willing to pay the rents required to carry the projects. It sold its suburban land, undeveloped, and instead put its efforts into building a model development, Spruce Court, on one of its urban sites, in working-class Cabbagetown.[15]

Spruce Court was to be the answer to the inhumane housing that working people found in the Ward. The complex had solid, well-built brick buildings; open, grassy common spaces; individual entrances; airy, well-ventilated, well-lit interiors; modern gas stoves and electric fixtures; and careful detailing throughout. Toronto Housing Company's 1915 publication, *Cottage Flats*, explained that 'sanitary conveniences, adequate bedroom accommodation and domestic privacy are the primary requirements for proper housing.' The small one-bedroom 'cottage flats' – today we call them duplexes – started at $14.50 a month; the large four-bedroom, two-storey units could cost as much as $29.00 a month, depending on their size and location. But despite the subsidies, they were too pricey to lure most workingmen. The landlords insisted on tough terms, moreover, that further discouraged families of modest means: rents had to be paid in advance, and large families couldn't occupy small units. Repeated increases led to rents that took as much as half the tenants' income, aiding the landlord's bottom line but forcing the blue-collar workers out. Even so, the company couldn't make a go of it. In the mid-1930s, during the Great Depression, it shut its doors[16] without ever having made an important contribution. All told, the Toronto Housing Company built some 260 units in two projects, Spruce Court and Riverdale Court, a minuscule proportion of Toronto's housing stock.

Another public-spirited agency, the Toronto Housing Commission, similarly failed to accomplish its social goal, in its case to build homes that would 'cater exclusively to the workingman.' Despite above-average quality and subsidies that lowered the cost of a home to about $4,000, about $1,000 less than the market price would be, most workingman found the homes beyond their reach. In the end, the commission sold the subsidized homes to the general public.

As a result of the failures of the Toronto Housing Commission and the Toronto Housing Company, social reformers came to believe that social housing, to be efficient, needed to be done on a large scale. The leader of the new thinking was Ontario's lieutenant-governor, Herbert A. Bruce, who perhaps more than anyone else set in train the country's embrace of public housing. Bruce made his historic housing debut on 6 March 1934, on the occasion of Toronto's one hundredth anniversary. Speaking before Prime Minister Bennett and other dignitaries at a celebratory luncheon, Bruce shocked his audience by deploring the misery in Toronto's slums: The only worthwhile centennial project, he insisted, was 'a plan that would recognize the inalienable right of every man and woman and child to a decent and dignified and healthful environment.'

Toronto's slums were indeed heavily populated during the Depression. During the 1920s, Toronto's suburbs had tried to provide more services than was prudent, leading to large tax increases by the suburban governments and to defaults by many residents. The desperate financial situation in the suburbs only became more serious after the Depression hit. In the end, a great many suburbanites abandoned the Toronto suburbs, coming to Toronto. Although jobs were scarce everywhere, the city offered casual work that allowed people to get by, and the ability to search for work on foot, avoiding the cost of public transit. The city also offered better living quarters, thanks to the rapid rate at which Torontonians freed up space in their own houses for tenants, to earn the revenue they needed to carry their households. In the 1930s, Torontonians converted an astonishing 22 per cent of the city's single-family dwellings to multiple occupancy, ten times the rate at which suburban homes were converted.[17]

These Depression-era conversions provided revenue for Toronto residents and opportunities for those abandoning the suburbs, but to the reformers, the cramped living conditions conjured up moral rot and social decay. Simply renovating a slum would not do, believed prominent reformers such as Humphrey Carver: 'It is as unwise as ever it was to put new wine into old bottles; a repaired slum still remains a slum.'[18] Bruce was likewise uncompromising. Referring to the lodger evil and its danger to the British stock, he cast the decision for society as whether to encourage sickness and sin or strength and saintliness: 'Let us make no mistake about that. It is only a question whether we shall house them in hospitals, mental institutions, reformatories and jails, or whether we shall house them in cleanly, light and sanitary surroundings where both body and soul will have a chance.'[19]

Bruce's luncheon speech led the city to ask him to produce a report – his *Report of the Lieutenant-Governor's Committee on Housing Conditions*, completed later that year. Despite the gains that had been made through the demolition of slum structures in the 1910s, it explained, poverty, overcrowding, and deteriorating conditions had come back, especially in the downtown core where many large single family dwellings had been converted into multi-family dwellings. Bruce warned that poor housing created 'a psychological problem. When privacy is too much interfered with, overcrowding may be said to exist. The breakdown of family life upon the introduction of another family into the dwelling unit is almost inevitable.' The city responded to his call for action with the Standard of Housing Bylaw, to encourage further demolition of substandard housing. The federal government also responded, with the *Dominion Housing Act*, the first of many pieces of legislation that would increasingly bring the federal government into the housing business.[20]

Bruce had an enticing argument for a country reeling with unemployment. Given enough economies of scale, haphazard, high-density housing could be economically replaced with more humane, low-density housing, kick-starting industry and putting people back to work.

> If the private builders are to get the greatest commercial benefits from the operations of this scheme, then the building must be on a large scale. Whole blocks of new houses, 100 or 1,000 at the same place and at the same time must be erected, and not costly and sporadic substitution of new houses for old in isolated places at diverse times. Then for the first time in the history of Canada, sufficient inducement will be offered a municipal or private housing corporation, to engage in the large-scale erection of real homes for low-wage earners. They will be assured of economic rents for every building by the tenants' own payments of rent, plus whatever contribution is necessary from the state fund. Can you imagine the vital, healthy stimulus such a scheme would give to employment?

Bruce was espousing the economic theories popular among the socialists of that era, that government construction projects would simultaneously take people off welfare while providing needed amenities. The result would be costless housing that also eradicated slums and strengthened the moral fibre of the populace.

> At this very time money is going into relief at the rate of between $400,000 and $500,000 a month. That is, let us say, at a conservative estimate $5,000,000 a year in relief. No wheels are set in motion by this. Nothing productive is done. It does not stimulate employment. And yet a housing program would most certainly save a part of this relief bill together with a part

of the rent bill which I mentioned a moment ago. If, taking the very lowest estimate, every house that was built during one year gave employment to one man during one year, and half the men employed were previously unemployed; or suppose the same number would obtain employment either in construction or in taking the places of those who would be brought into construction, this would mean that the city would save the relief of 1,000 families every year during the five years during which the building program continued. This is the lowest possible estimate. At the end of it all there would be something to show for the money expended, something accomplished ...

The members of the Housing Centre are in favour of subsidizing low-cost housing and slum clearance. They are opposed to any piecemeal building or rebuilding of dwellings in any part of the city without careful consideration of the present and future needs of each district as a whole and of the entire city as a unit. They believe that the carrying out of these aims would provide widespread employment, lessen the burden of relief, and improve the health and morale of the many, many families who are now depressed and weakened by the conditions under which they live. You will notice, therefore, that what I have said today might be termed a plan of action by which these necessary, these superlatively important objectives can be achieved.[21]

The ultimate objective for the members of the Housing Centre and other reformers was the preservation of the family and the Anglo-Saxon way of life. As Carver explained the benefits of bringing housing into the modern age, 'the mechanization of household equipment and the economy of bedroom space to be cleaned would help to liberate the housewife from the monotonous servitude of domestic chores and allow her to develop family life in more fruitful directions.' Likewise, another prominent advocate of social housing, Albert Rose, praised plans for what would become Canada's largest public housing project, Regent Park North, for promoting 'maternal efficiency.'[22]

The model housing that Bruce proposed as a remedy to the slums of Toronto would be built,[23] to wide applause: awards and international recognition would follow. But rather than produce the model citizen that Bruce envisaged, the public housing projects soon became crime-ridden and degenerate, their courtyards derelict and blots upon the landscape. Neither did the financial benefits materialize, nor affordable housing for the masses. To the contrary, the new era of planned housing developments, along with health regulations, had the unwanted effect of making homebuilding more difficult and expensive, leading to increased costs and a restricted supply of housing. The hardship fell especially on the poor.

Only decades later would the consequences of taking the initiative out of the hands of individuals become clear to analysts. A study sponsored by the federal government's Canada Mortgage and Housing Corporation found that the regulatory apparatus that began early in the century 'began to impede incremental housing development. By mid-century, development practices were beginning to exclude the more modest owner-builder, grow-as-you-go solution, in favour of new, fully planned and serviced developments. In the relatively rapid shift from unplanned to planned housing development, a housing process accessible to a wide range of income groups was replaced with a housing product for affluent households. Depending on interest rates, households below the 50th and 60th income percentile lost the option of developing their own properties gradually.'[24]

5 Canada's War Effort against the Cities

Toronto's social reformers had counterparts in Canada's other major cities and all had a steadfast ally in the federal government, which also strove to reduce the urban population. From confederation in 1867 on, the chief activity of the federal government had been attracting immigrants and opening up the wilderness through gifts of crown land, homesteading grants, and building a trans-Canada railway, among other policies. But much of the public acted at cross purposes to the federal government: Although the federal government was encouraging rural settlement, farmers were increasingly leaving the land for cities. By the late nineteenth century, this exodus had become large, frustrating federal plans to develop the country's vast natural resources.

Early in the twentieth century, the federal government had another reason, too, to discourage people from locating in cities. The labour movement was successfully unionizing urban workers in Montreal, Toronto, Winnipeg, and other cities, leading to hundreds of strikes involving hundreds of thousands of workers during the First World War and its immediate aftermath.[1] Following the Russian Revolution in 1917, the cities became even greater hotbeds of labour activism. Toronto's May Day celebration at Broadway Hall on Spadina Avenue invited 'Men and Women Who Work in the Factory, Mill or Workshop' to 'celebrate our Russian comrades' glorious victory in the overthrow of the barbarous despotism of Russian Nobility ... With the international solidarity of labour established, then , and only then, will liberty triumph.'[2]

Canada's political leaders feared social unrest. Business, too, was alarmed. *Industrial Canada*, the organ of the Canadian Manufacturers' Association, cautioned that 'Out of the slums stalk the Socialist with his red flag, the Union agitator with the auctioneer's voice and the Anarchist with his torch.'[3]

The end of the war provided our government with an opportunity to restore the nation's course of rural development. With the nation's 600,000 servicemen homeward bound, the government decided in 1917 to create the *Soldier Settlement Act: An Act to Assist Returned Soldiers in Settling upon the Land and to Increase Agricultural Production*.[4] Apart from encouraging veterans to move to the countryside, the government also hoped to promote social stability in the strike-torn cities. 'We believe that we cannot better fortify this country against the waves of unrest and discontent ... than by making the greatest possible proportion of the soldiers of our country settlers upon the land,' stated Minister of the Interior Arthur Meighen, in introducing a revised *Soldier Settlement Act* to the House of Commons in 1919. That same year, as acting minister of justice, Meighen also helped suppress the Winnipeg General Strike.

The *Soldier Settlement Act* awarded land grants of up to 160 acres to veterans, generally at little or no cost.[5] An article by C.W. Cavers of the Soldier Settlement Board in the *Regina Morning Leader*, entitled 'Army of Men Placed on Prairie Farms by Soldier Settlement: Saskatchewan Stands Second in the Dominion in the Number of Veteran Farmers with more than 3,000,' describes the scale of the undertaking and the government's rationale:[6]

> Saskatchewan offers a very excellent field for this great experiment. It has considerable land of good quality yet to be developed. Taking advantage of the wide powers of the Act, the Soldier Settlement Board has made progress in the direction of bringing under cultivation large areas of desirable farm land which have been contained in Indian and Forest Reserves and also portions that had been held by Doukhobors. Many of these rich agricultural lands were during the past season made available for soldier settlement. In the case of the Indian Reserves they were purchased from the Indians at a valuation,[7] divided into farm units and sold to returned soldiers at cost ...
>
> In addition to these large areas which are available for soldier settlement, the Board disposed of to returned soldiers 10,000 acres of Doukhobor lands near Kamsck, and 27,000 acres of Hudson Bay, lands in various parts of the province. The development of these tracts as well as many acres of idle lands formerly owned by private individuals means a decided fillip to the expansion of our great West and increase of the coun-

try's resources. It means that thousands of young men who would have been compelled to seek employment in the cities, which are already overcrowded to the neglect of the agricultural interests of Canada will have become producers in the truest sense because of the extremely favorable terms of the Soldier Settlement Act.

The *Soldier Settlement Act* disproportionately settled veterans in the prairies and other areas where 'by reason of lands remaining undeveloped, agricultural production is being retarded,' and it gave its Soldier Settlement Board sweeping powers to determine what land was suitable for seizure for settlement.[8] But the act would settle only 25,000 veterans – most returning veterans did not want the life of a farmer – and it was widely viewed as a failure, even among those who decided to accept the government's land. Many of the farms had poor soil, many veterans lacked farm experience, and, saddled with large debts, many veterans soon found themselves in difficulty.[9]

When the Second World War broke out, the federal government did not want to fail its veterans again. The government needed consistently good land if it was to further an agricultural society, but little was available. To overcome this shortcoming, the government decided to expropriate Indian lands, despite its treaty obligations. As described by the 1966 Royal Commission on Aboriginal Peoples in *Looking Forward, Looking Back*:

> By the middle of the war years, veterans and bureaucrats were already considering how more lands could be obtained for returning Canadian veterans. As early as 1943, H. Allen, Edmonton district superintendent, had corresponded with W.G. Murchison, director of soldier settlement, on the subject of securing Indian reserve lands:
>
> There is one department of which our minister Mr. Crerar is the head who do have surplus land on their hands from time to time, i.e. the Department of Indian Affairs ... Some of these lands are the finest in the district in which they are situated. I particularly refer to Saddle Lake near St. Paul, Fairview and Berwyn in the Peace River district, the Blackfoot reserve near Gleichen, near Ponoka at Hobbema, and there are possibly others.
>
> Indian land at Saddle Lake was also being eyed by members of the Royal Canadian Legion at St. Paul, who wrote to the IAB [Indian Affairs Branch] in 1944 urging that this good Indian land, guaranteed by treaty, be set aside for returning veterans. However, T.A. Crerar, minister of mines

and resources and therefore responsible for the IAB, informed the St. Paul Legion that the Saddle Lake Indians had little enough land left, having surrendered 18,720 acres to the Soldier Settlement Board after the first war. Crerar therefore turned down that request, but the IAB did approve the surrender of 7,924 acres in the Fort St. John area, at a bargain price of less than $9 per acre. The land purchased in the west after the Second World War was pooled with land that still remained from major surrenders for First World War soldier settlement, to be made available once again to returning soldiers.'[10]

Apart from the failure to provide First World War veterans with good land, the *Soldier Settlement Act* of 1919 had also failed, it was widely believed, in its over-emphasis on full-time farming. This time, under new legislation entitled the *Veterans Land Act*, the government permitted part-time farms on the urban fringe, to enable veterans to combine farm activity with city jobs. The preamble to the act explained that agriculture would rehabilitate veterans, that part-time farming coupled with employment was 'an increasingly important aspect of rural and semi-rural life in Canada,' and that it was in the public interest to help veterans become owners of 'farm homes,' since most veterans had few assets.[11]

The government would not, however, encourage veterans to live within cities. To the contrary, the act's part-time farming, or small-holdings, provisions were designed to lure urban veterans to the farm – to 'bonus' the veteran out of the city into the country, as put in 1950 by Milton Gregg, the minister of veterans affairs.[12] The drafters of the legislation had familiar reasons for keeping veterans out of the city: They held farming in high regard and they were preoccupied with maintaining public order. Among the act's chief framers was Robert England, from 1940 to 1942 the executive secretary of the General Advisory Committee on Demobilization and Rehabilitation, which shaped the package of benefits that became the Veterans Charter. England, who sat on the subcommittee that drafted the *Veterans Land Act*, wrote in the fall of 1942 that the *Veterans Land Act* would promote social stability and stave off the union movement: 'the independence of the man of the soil has ever reflected the area of personal freedom that attaches to the agriculturalist who owns his farm. There is here a social value, a check to the uniformity and the proletarianization of urbanism.' Both the full- and part-time farming provisions were designed, he wrote, to 'encourage a non-urban settlement.' Part-time farming would combine 'the socially desirable objective of rural home ownership and some decentralization.'[13]

Other framers of the *Veterans Land Act*, such as Gordon Murchison, the director of Soldier Settlement, also sought to encourage wage-earning veterans to discover the virtues of rural living. Murchison, a Saskatchewan native who crafted the government's Second World War model for land settlement, viewed small holdings as a 'safety valve' deflecting those 'not wholly suited for full-time agriculture' towards a viable alternative.[14] As well, some saw the small-holdings provisions as a safety net should Canada's economy turn sour after he war. Several subcommittee members referred to Great Depression subsistence projects that took families off relief.

The government passed the *Veterans' Land Act* in 1942, with some servicemen already homebound. The Defence Department's 1943 manual on a soldier's rights and responsibilities, *The Canadian Soldier's Handbook of General Information*, describes the government's role in helping soldiers re-establish themselves after the war:

> You are probably looking forward to the day when victory has been won and you can resume your former occupation. The following notes are designed to tell you what the Government is doing towards re-establishing you in the event of your discharge during this war and also after your discharge at the end of the war ...
>
> Land Settlement
>
> The Veterans' Land Act, 1942, is a flexible measure. It provides wide scope for those of you who are interested in settling on the land. The advantages of this Land Act will be available according to your experience, general fitness and desire to settle on the land or obtain a home in a rural district. There is provision for three types of settlement: (a) full-time farming for men with practical experience in farm operation; (b) small holding settlement – which means a rural home and small acreage located close to employment opportunity, where the main source of revenue is from industrial or other employment; (c) small holding settlement coupled with commercial fishing for veterans experienced in the business of fishing in Canada's coastal regions or inland districts where fishing is engaged in on a commercial basis.
>
> The object of this Act is to enable you to acquire rural home ownership within your active working years and to maintain a reasonable standard of living for yourself and family. The State assistance therefore takes the form of a loan and conditional grant which are reflected in a contract between yourself and the Government whereby the Government absorbs at the outset a substantial part of the cost of the enterprise.

Settlement under this Act is a joint undertaking. The State bears a large proportion of the cost of a wide variety of settlement establishments and you are expected to assume certain responsibilities in the settlement agreement. In addition to the necessary qualifications to participate in settlement, is provision by you of a down payment of ten percent of the cost of the land and improvements. This down payment will vary from approximately $200 to $360 according to the type of individual settlement, and the annual payment will vary from approximately $90 to $145 over a 25-year period.'[15]

The *Veterans Land Act* provided inexpensive houses for returning veterans and the families of those killed in the war. To drum up popular support for the program at home before war's end, the government then widely touted its benefits through a media campaign. 'Home Ownership – In Town or Suburb: How Canada's Veterans Benefit,' ran one 1944 ad in Toronto's *Globe and Mail*.

A home of their own is the dream of most Canadians – and the dream, particularly of those, far from home, fighting on the sea, on land, or in the air. To some, a home means a place, away from the city, where there is good earth for raising vegetables, where there is room for a few chickens, some flowers, perhaps some fruit trees and where the children can grow up in a country atmosphere. To others a home means, first of all, city advantages, schools nearby for the children, and a short run in the morning to office or work. No matter which is the ambition of the ex-service man or ex-service woman, Canada's rehabilitation program can assist them in it.[16]

The 'city advantages' that the ad referred to, could only be had by those commuting to work from the suburbs. 'This Act, planned to give a new meaning to land settlement, suits the veterans who want land with their home. It provides generous assistance in financing homes for city and other workers on small acreages, outside the high taxation area.' Toronto-area servicemen who had already returned to civilian life were invited to visit the local Veterans' Welfare Office. All readers were asked to 'SEND THIS ADVERTISEMENT TO SOME MAN OR WOMAN OVERSEAS,' and invited to request a pamphlet entitled 'Back to Civil Life.'

Although the newspaper ads gave towns and suburbs equal billing, the government expected most applicants to settle in farming and fishing communities. To its great surprise, most sought financing as smallholders, typically on the fringes of cities.[17] Of the more than 140,000 veterans who applied for grants and loans as full-time farmers, commercial fishermen or smallholders,[18] more than 100,000 received financing to allow them to settle as smallholders. Only in the prairies did most applicants choose full-time farming. In all other regions of the country, between 80 per cent and 90 per cent chose to be small-holders. In Ontario, 87.5 per cent chose small-holdings, disproportionately near Toronto's booming economy.[19]

Because the government hoped that veterans who settled outside cities would commute to industrial work in the cities and also farm part-time, administrators decreed that veterans ought to acquire building lots of at least two acres in area, the minimum believed necessary for commercial farming. Two acres could accommodate three pigs; three acres a cow. Also to promote a farming environment, administrators typically required that building lots be scattered, rather than in compact suburban subdivisions.[20] Veterans became subject to an interview that required them to explain how they planned to use their land. Most would pay lip-service to their intention to farm part-time.

In 1943 and 1944, anticipating the end of the war, administrators acquired land for rural part-time farm settlements on the outskirts of cities. Their plans were soon derailed, however, as the flood of returning servicemen created a housing crisis. In 1945 the federal cabinet established a high-level Interdepartmental Housing Committee,[21] chaired by the minister of finance, to speed house construction. At its first meeting, it decided to have the *Veterans Land Act* administrators build houses on half-acre lots, rather than the two-acres or larger lots originally envisaged.[22]

Veterans snapped up the half-acre lots on the outskirts of cities and began to ask why they couldn't have land within cities.[23] In October 1945 the Canadian Legion argued in a brief to the Special Committee on Veterans Affairs[24] that veterans everywhere suffered 'extremely unsatisfactory' circumstances and that 'it is quite obvious that a need can be met by the extension of the Act to cover urban housing.' Sympathetic parliamentarians from all parties then carried the fight to the House of Commons. Thomas Kidd, a Conservative MP from Kingston, represented the views of many when he argued, during a long debate on 1 August 1946, that 'the boys do not want' to settle in unserviced fringe areas. But Ian A. Mackenzie, the minister of veterans affairs, would not countenance the urban housing that parliamentarians, and the veterans themselves, so clearly demanded. 'If you admit the principle of urban housing under the Veterans Land Act ... you destroy the fundamental feature of that act, which is farm settlement,' he argued, adding that 'real settlement' meant 'real farming.'[25]

The debate would be settled, and opponents of urban settlements would have their way, once C.D. Howe, the all-powerful Minister of Everything,[26] decided to bar housing loans under the *Veterans Land Act* in subdivisions of more than six dwellings. While he was at it, Howe also barred loans in areas with any population to speak of, including cities whose population exceeded 5,000 and the outskirts of urban areas with more than 15,000 people. These measures, he stated, had 'arrested a trend towards the small holdings section becoming a vehicle for financing veterans housing.'

The government disqualified urban housing on the grounds that the *National Housing Act* already made home ownership available on 'easy terms.'[27] In fact, the *National Housing Act* offered nothing to most veterans. As Murchison put it in 1945, the average veteran's financial position meant that he 'cannot possibly participate under the National Housing Act.' His successor, T.J. Rutherford, stated that VLA dwellings 'represent the best value of any houses being built at the present time.' The minister of veterans affairs, Ian Mackenzie, confirmed the land act's generous terms, telling the House of Commons that 'our terms are much more favourable' than those of the alternatives, including heavily subsidized housing provided by other government departments.

Veterans stood to benefit by acceding to the government's desire to promote a rural economy, yet most veterans declined. Only 10 per cent of veterans had an agricultural background, by the government's own reckoning, and even among this group, many were too young to have worked on the land and many who had worked the land wanted a different future. Canada's returning servicemen overwhelmingly saw their future as urbanites, and resented being coerced by government policy to either accept unpalatable housing or forgo a major benefit.[28] When they could take advantage of loopholes, they often did. For example, because disabled veterans were exempt from the two-acre rule, many talked their physicians into providing them with a certificate vouching that they were at least 50 per cent disabled, which allowed them to build on smaller 'city-sized' lots.[29]

In the end, the *Veterans Land Act* would finance over 100,000 postwar families in small-holdings,[30] representing perhaps 500,000 Canadians, and it would have historic consequences for the future of settlement in Canada.[31] By giving veterans who had come from the farm a choice between land on the farm and land near cities, many rural veterans obtained an opportunity to leave the farm. At the same time, the lure of subsidized land drew city veterans to the city's outskirts. The result would help create, and help populate, the modern suburb.

Yet, as generous as the land act was, and as significant as it was in shaping postwar suburban development, its consequences could have been far more dramatic. They were not only because the land act wasn't quite generous enough to pull people out of cities. In testimony before the Standing Committee on National Defence and Veterans Affairs, the following short exchange between MP George Proud and H. Clifford Chadderton, Chairman of the National Council of Veteran Associations in Canada, sums it up:

> George Proud: Because only ten percent of veterans ever applied for Veterans' Land Act, for instance.
>
> Clifford Chadderton: Oh yes. Of course, the reason for that is with the Veterans' Land Act and its sister, the small holdings program, there weren't very many veterans who wanted to go back to the farm or try to make a living in small holdings. I think that was the answer.[32]

6 CMHC and Cheap Financing Open Up the Suburbs

In addition to creating the *Veterans Land Act*, the federal government created the Central Mortgage and Housing Corporation, a permanent civilian agency, to provide housing after the war.[1] 'We were going to call it the Central Mortgage Corporation with no reference to housing at all,' recalled David B. Mansur, its first president. 'But later, in a meeting with Finance Minister J.L. Ilsley, Dr. McIntosh proposed a change. "I think it should be called Central Mortgage and Housing Corporation," he said, "because they're going to be in the housing business and no fooling." Of course, he was right.'[2]

The large number of returning servicemen weighed heavily on government thinking. As Mansur explained: 'As the war ended, everybody knew there was going to be a housing problem. We had a million people in the armed forces, and there just wasn't enough housing for them as they returned to civilian life ... Clearly, the government needed a new agency to help deal with the problem.'

CMHC's first responsibilities involved managing the major housing programs that governments had undertaken during the war, in aid of the war effort. With the country's great need for city workers, governments had reversed policies that discriminated against urban housing, leading to record levels of Canadian workers, many of whom had come from rural areas, in the munitions factories. But these workers faced a severe housing shortage, especially in Toronto, because little housing had been built during the depression of the 1930s.[3] The federal government stepped in to become 'the major player on the local scene.'[4] It offered grants that encouraged property owners to convert their dwellings into rooming houses,[5] it administered an Emergency Shelter Program to aid some 16,000 war veterans' families without a permanent place to live,[6] and, more importantly, it constructed large tracts of housing in the townships around Toronto through Wartime Housing Corporation. During the 1940s, this crown corporation, which CMHC took over after the war, built some 50,000 rental houses, most of them single-family residences, for war workers, for returning veterans, and for the families of those killed in the war.[7] The legacy of Wartime Housing's activities – spartan, one-and-a-half storey bungalows with pitched roofs that CMHC sold in the early 1950s[8] – remains in the working-class suburbs of Toronto and other cities across Canada.

The CMHC did more than manage and wind up the federal government's intervention as a wartime housing developer. It became the dominant force in peacetime housing, in everything from setting housing standards to financing housing to acting as the actual developer. In the process, it became the chief instrument of government housing policies, profoundly changing existing settlement patterns by opening up the countryside to development.[9]

The expansive agency that became the CMHC had its origins in federal government housing policies that preceded the war. In 1935 the federal government created the *Dominion Housing Act*, its first major housing legislation, to subsidize home ownership and kick start the economy. With this act, the federal government formally began its long history of subsidizing home ownership over rental accommodation and low-density over compact development. As a result, people could buy larger homes on larger lots than otherwise, they would less often need to finance their home purchase by renting out space in their homes, and they would become owners, rather than renters, at a younger age than otherwise.[10]

Before the government entered the mortgage business, Canadians arranged their own financing privately, generally without benefit of large institutions, which tended to consider residential mortgages too risky. A study of vacant lots sold in Toronto in the 1910s found that, in working class districts, the majority of purchasers paid in cash, and that when they did arrange financing, the source tended to be individual lenders or the developers, who commonly offered 'easy terms' to encourage business.[11] Institutional lenders – typically life insurance or loan and trust companies – provided mortgages for a small proportion of lots in working-class neighbourhoods, usually 10 to 20 per cent, depending on the neighbourhood. In tonier districts such as Lawrence Park, institutional lenders financed one-third of the lots. In the purchase of developed lots, where houses were already built, the poor less often paid cash, and more often relied on private lenders. Here institutional lenders played an even smaller role in financing the housing of the poor.

Mortgage terms were tough before the *Dominion Housing Act* legislation took effect. Home purchasers needed to provide down payments of at least 40 per cent of the property's value, mortgages lasted but five years and, if institutional lenders became risk averse, they were under no obligation to renew the mortgages. The *Dominion Housing Act* changed the housing marketplace. It doubled the term of the mortgage to ten years and halved the down payment to 20 per cent by topping up the private lender mortgages with government loans at below-market interest rates that covered 20 per cent of a home's assessed value. Through these joint loans, part from the public sector, part from the private sector, the act accomplished its purpose – 'to create more housing and, through economic levering, accelerate the recovery from the Great Depression.'[12] To entice private lenders into dealing with prospective homeowners who were otherwise poor credit risks, 'the federal government agreed to compensate the lenders for default losses on a fairly generous basis free of charge. For example, two-thirds of the losses incurred in the first eight years of the loan were borne by the federal government.'[13]

The legislation's 'economic levering,' which was designed to provide jobs in the construction industry,[14] acted to promote suburban development, primarily for the affluent. A study of the homes that it financed in its first four years shows more than two-thirds of mortgage recipients to be professionals, managers, or business owners who mostly built large, expensive homes in Forest Hill and affluent districts in Etobicoke, Scarborough, and Leaside. More than 80 per cent of *Dominion Housing Act*-financed homes, in fact, were located in the suburbs, and much of the rest were built in the city's outlying districts. Along with other government initiatives, such as the 1937 *Federal Home Improvement Loans Guarantee Act*,[15] the government aimed to inculcate a home owning rather than a renting ethic: the government called it a 'house-conscious feeling.'[16] All told, reported F.W. Nicolls, the federal government's director of housing, 'we find that approximately 40 per cent of our residential construction was financed with Government assistance.'[17]

In 1938, the government created the Central Mortgage Bank as a subsidiary of the Bank of Canada to cover the many unserviceable mortgages, most of them to farmers, that existed at the end of the Great Depression. The Central Mortgage Bank was a bailout agency that allowed lending companies to rewrite their bad loans to 80 per cent of their fair current value and at current interest rates. The Central Mortgage Bank would then absorb half of the losses using its $200 million in capital – a substantial amount for those days – and the power to borrow. Operating in this way through the loan and trust companies, the bank maintained an adequate supply of capital for farmers and others in need of residential mortgages.[18]

The Central Mortgage Bank was dismantled in August 1939, with the advent of war, to be resurrected as the Central Mortgage and Housing Corporation in 1946. In part, CMHC was charged with promoting the development of remote areas by subsidizing private lenders (then primarily life insurance companies) to go far afield. 'To ensure maximum availability of joint loans in every community across Canada, the lenders were paid cost allowances and travel expenses to make less profitable loans in small and remote communities,' CMHC states.[19] But even with these inducements, the private sector found servicing remote areas inefficient and unprofitable relative to the business environment that existed in urban areas. 'We had a dreadful time in the early years getting lending institutions to make loans in remote areas. They didn't want to send employees into the hinterland to make one or two loans. It just wasn't economical,' said, David Mansur, who led the corporation from 1946 to 1954.

CMHC's inability to coax the private sector into the hinterlands, and into risky loans to low-income Canadians, led it to enter the mortgage business more forcefully, by dealing directly with homeowners. The federal government thus became the lender of last resort. Explained CMHC president Jean-Claude Villiard: 'Much like a central bank, CMHC was authorized to make direct mortgage loans funded by federal dollars, when, in the opinion of the Corporation, joint loans were not available to potential borrowers, including those living in remote or rural communities as well as those living in mining or single-industry towns.'[20] Federal funds at that point accounted for one-quarter of all the joint-lending in the country.

But CMHC, even with its government-backed borrowing ability, could not muster enough financing for the housing boom it wished to see. For that, it needed to convince the banks to get into the residential business, a sector in which they had neither experience nor interest.[21] The need for bank involvement became all the more pressing when the post-war baby boom period also delivered high immigration: from 15,000 immigrants in 1945, immigration shot up to 221,000 by 1952.

Banks preferred to lend to businesses, where loans were liquid. To overcome the banks' resistance, the federal government intervened yet again with a package generous enough to entice the chartered banks. Under the 1954 *National Housing Act*, banks would provide government mortgage loans while CMHC made mortgages liquid by guaranteeing a marketplace; CMHC would buy or sell residential mortgages and, for good measure, would insure them, too, to allay banks' fears of making loans on properties with low down payments to poor credit risks. The legislation did the trick. In one year the number of new loans jumped by more than a third, and between 1954 and 1956, although the banks continued to be wary, they nevertheless provided mortgages for more than half of the homes built under the *National Housing Act*.[22] 'By the early 1950s, loans representing $93\frac{1}{3}$ per cent of the lending value of the property became available,' the agency explained. 'In an effort to keep the borrowing cost at the lowest possible levels, the interest rates on some joint loans were set at no more than two percent above the yield on 12-year Canada Bonds.'[23] Through such mechanisms, CMHC came to finance one in three homes in Canada.

Although CMHC operated throughout Canada, its activities centred on the outskirts of cities. As a City of Toronto study described the opening up of the suburbs, 'Federal legislation made it easier for developers to build houses and for home-owners to buy them. It was now economically viable for developers to build on a much grander scale, creating entire subdivisions rather than just a few homes for resale.'[24]

CMHC became a hands-on, can-do, all-purpose builder-developer-financier with stunning results. One description of the time describes CMHC's micro-management capabilities in creating Lawrence Manor, which had been farmland from the early 1800s until the 1940s.

> CMHC serviced this entire subdivision putting in water service, sewers, and roads, before selling off individual lots to a number of small builders in the early 1950's. The first Lawrence Manor buyers had to qualify for a CMHC mortgage. These mortgages were for 25 years at a rate of only four and a half percent!
>
> Cows were still grazing on the north-west corner of Bathurst Street and Lawrence Avenue in 1951 when the first residents began moving into this neighbourhood. Lawrence Plaza was built on the site of this former cow patch in 1960. Lawrence Plaza was the largest shopping centre in Toronto, when it first opened. It attracted shoppers from all over Toronto and helped put the Lawrence Manor neighbourhood on the map.[25]

CMHC provides another description of its sweeping role in transforming Canadian society: 'CMHC helped create entire cities, such as Ajax, Ontario and Gander, Newfoundland. Thousands of storey-and-a-half houses across Canada were built by CMHC in the years following the war, bringing about new neighbourhoods, towns and cities. In the absence of a co-ordinated building industry, CMHC stepped in to deal with every aspect of housing: servicing land, building and selling housing and arranging mortgage financing.'[26]

CMHC needed to 'step in' because, otherwise, precious little development would have occurred outside cities, and housing would have followed a trend that governments did not favour. 'The life insurance companies preferred to put their money into large rental projects of two or three hundred units,' stated David Mansur. 'Loans like that were much cheaper to administer. The trust and loan companies didn't like National Housing Act loans at all. They were too long term for their purposes.'[27] Rather than the urban houses and major rental projects that the private sector lenders favoured, Canada's public sector lender would fabricate communities outside cities that the federal government favoured.[28]

7 Partial Amalgamation, Full Sprawl

WITH SATISH DHAR

The federal government's efforts to encourage people to settle outside Toronto's borders after the Second World War were in some ways ham-handed failures. Because the *Veterans Land Act* required returning servicemen to settle outside cities to qualify for the generous land grants on offer, only 10 per cent bothered to apply. Despite CMHC's incentives to private developers, and to private lenders, the private housing market remained reluctant to open up the suburbs.

Yet the government, in the end, had all the success it needed. The 10 per cent that the *Veterans Land Act* would provide boosted the outskirts of Toronto by some 100,000 residents, an amount equivalent to three times the postwar population of Toronto's largest suburb, North York.[1] The CMHC, by assuming most of the private sector's business risk and becoming a hands-on real estate developer in its own right, would be responsible for many more. Other federal programs, plus those at the provincial level, likewise redirected people from city to suburb.[2] The population of Toronto's suburbs almost doubled between 1945 and 1953, rising by 94 per cent; the City of Toronto's population, meanwhile, stagnated, falling by 2 per cent.[3]

The suburban expansion, although it had been long in preparation, was nevertheless rife with unwanted consequences. While governments provided enough in subsidies to convince Canadians to relocate to the suburbs, governments didn't provide enough in subsidies to finance the infrastructure that the suburbanites would need. The result was substandard conditions serious enough to threaten future development.

North York, for example, lacked central sewage facilities. There, 15,000 septic tanks were built in impervious clay soil, preventing human wastes from either evaporating or being absorbed into the soil and leaving the sewage nowhere to go. In other suburbs, overloaded sewage plants discharged partially treated effluents into streams and channels that flowed into the Humber and Don rivers, turning them into open sewers. In 1949 a report by the engineering firm of Gore and Storrie warned that the inadequate sewerage system put 'serious limitations on the development of new residential areas.'[4] By the early 1950s the lack of proper sewage facilities had become a public health hazard.[5]

The governments' push to the suburbs had also neglected to provide for adequate supplies of drinking water. The new subdivisions relied on wells that often produced poor quality water, and often ran dangerously low. In North York, water rationing became a feature of suburban life, with families visiting Toronto friends to bathe amid stories of parents resorting to bathing babies in ginger ale. North York restricted outdoor watering for nine summers in a row, causing grass and flowers to burn.[6] Neither were suburban roads satisfactory. They were poorly maintained and lacked connections across ravines and rivers, rendering travel between the suburbs and the city inconvenient and time-consuming.[7] Public transit, meanwhile, ran along few routes, providing rudimentary service that was uncoordinated with the city's Toronto Transportation Commission.[8]

Similarly, the suburbs had failing grades in education. In many of the suburbs surrounding Toronto, where couples had moved to raise their children, public education expenditure consumed a larger proportion of the municipal budget than in the city. Yet the money spent per pupil was lower than in the city, leading to larger classes taught by less qualified teachers in poorly equipped schools.[9] Suburbs 'were unable to provide their children with a minimum standard of education except with the utmost financial difficulty,' explained Frederick Gardiner, chair in the early 1950s of the Toronto and York Planning Board. More generally, some municipalities were unable to finance the services that their residential development required. 'The issuance of building permits were stopped or held up on account of the inability of some municipalities to provide the services required.'[10]

The problem came down to the tax base. The new suburbs did not have the industry[11] and the affluence necessary to provide their governments with the revenues required to fund needed services:

> In one municipality, North York, the population increased from less than 30,000 in 1945 to over 100,000 in 1953. It is what we call a dormitory municipality: The residents go there to live and elsewhere to work. It

developed into a residential area for people of moderate means. In the absence of industrial development, there was not sufficient assessment to provide within a reasonable tax rate water supply, sewage disposal, roads, sidewalks, lights and educational facilities for the children of the young families who settled within its boundaries. The situation was duplicated in a lesser degree in other suburban municipalities ...

When some of our municipalities had difficulty in selling their bonds it was evident that a major operation was necessary.[12]

The 'major operation' that Gardiner referred to was amalgamation. While the suburbs had the great infrastructure needs, they had little taxing ability. North York, the largest of the thirteen municipalities, had a mere 8 per cent of the Metro area's assessment base. Toronto, in contrast, had 62 per cent.[13] Toronto's infrastructure, moreover, was relatively robust, despite the decline it had experienced during the Depression and the war. Its system of water mains and pumping stations not only supplied water from Lake Ontario to the city's residents and businesses but also to some of the inner suburbs, including York and affluent Forest Hill.[14] Likewise, Toronto's underground sewers collected waste water from adjoining communities as well as its own territory, which it drained into two large treatment plants.

The extent to which the suburbs had inadequate infrastructure hit home slowly, sometimes when the volume of sewage from suburbs exceeded the city's capacity, sometimes when septic systems failed. Meanwhile, problems with transportation also became acute. 'The situation became desperate,' explained Gardiner. 'Our highways became plugged with motor vehicles. 300,000 motor vehicles are domiciled in the area and an additional 100,000 come in and go out each day.'

Seeing the increasingly 'desperate' situation that they had created, governments could have reacted in several ways. They could have stopped the expansion by removing the subsidies, preventing the difficulties from becoming more acute and making them more manageable. Or they could have enforced laws that prevented pollution of streams and groundwater by sewage,[15] making owners responsible for the adequacy of their septic systems and thus discouraging settlement where the costs of containing sewage was high. Governments did neither.

Instead, their answer to the suburbs' ill-planned expansion was better planning, on a larger scale. As Gardiner put it, 'nothing short of a unified municipality' could solve the metropolis's problems.[16] By integrating the city's infrastructure with that of the outskirts, not only would the whole be strengthened financially but a balkanized system could be rationalized. As it was, some suburbs could see insolvency looming and had begun to merge with each other or otherwise restructure themselves, just as some Toronto suburbs had in the 1920s and 1930s prior to their bankruptcy.[17] The logic of amalgamation seemed unassailable. Explained Gardiner:

> Over the 40 years from 1912 to 1952 the metropolitan area became divided into 13 separate municipalities composed of one city, three villages, four towns and five urbanized townships. Each was geared to a local pattern of development. None was very much concerned about what was happening to its neighbour and none was interested in the general and proper development of the whole area. With this impractical and unrealistic development something was bound to happen and it did not take it long to occur...
>
> The Toronto and York Planning Board, of which I was chairman for five years, lined its walls with plans for the development of the whole area. We knew what needed to be done but in the absence of power to tax the constituent municipalities and to take expropriation proceedings, none of the essential works could be undertaken.[18]

Gardiner resolved to change a system he had come to view as dysfunctional. Since 1942, as chair of a committee of the Toronto and York Roads Commission, he had been frustrated in his plans to build a highway system by the unwillingness of the many local municipalities and agencies to set aside their local powers and penny-pinching ways for the greater good. In 1945, as a member of a provincial committee on planning charged with meeting the province's capital infrastructure needs, he decided Ontario needed 'something in the nature of Joe Stalin's five-year plan' to ram through needed hospital construction. In 1947, as vice-chairman of the Toronto and York Planning Board, he found adamant opposition in suburban York County for his plans to build a unified system of arterial roads and a single public transit network.[19] In 1948, although the City of Toronto agreed to pay two-thirds of a greenbelt plan, York County refused to provide the remaining third.

Gardiner's views echoed through society. 'As officials in the 1940s planned the modernization of the city and the suburbanization of the surrounding countryside, they believed that local government needed more centralization and financial capability to develop roads, transit, sewers, and parks, as well as such services as health and welfare,' a history of the times reports.[20] The City of Toronto's 1943 master plan proposed 'a partnership of all the municipalities in the Metropolitan area' to develop the 'vacant land of the adjacent suburbs.' The premier of Ontario, Leslie Frost, favoured amalgamation, stating that 'the solution of the problem involves the unification of local governing bodies into one central administration.'[21] Eric Hardy, director of the Bureau of Municipal Research, concurred: 'From the point of view of administration, the arguments in favour of amalgamation, that is of complete unification, seem to me to be patent and obvious.'[22]

Most of all, the City of Toronto wanted amalgamation in order to arrest the slow decline that federal and provincial government policies had set in motion.[23] With Toronto's people and industries slowly migrating to the suburbs, the city was losing the levies that they had been providing. Suburbanites, too, were costing the city by using Toronto facilities – fire stations, roads, parks, policing – without contributing taxes for their upkeep. By absorbing the suburbs, the city reasoned, it could keep the tax revenues from its lost industry and gain suburbanites as taxpayers. It could also control the growth that would occur in the suburbs, to prevent uneconomic developments from undermining municipal finances. The city thus applied in 1950 to the Ontario Municipal Board, a provincial regulatory agency, for its amalgamation with twelve suburban municipalities.

The amalgamation request was denied, following fierce opposition from local governments that wanted to retain local autonomy.[24] Bowing to the local governments, Ontario's premier then opted for a half-way measure: 'I believed that partial amalgamation was the answer,' he said, in explaining Bill 80, the legislation that would restructure the region. For the city, it would be the worst of all conceivable outcomes. The partial amalgamation that took place would deplete the city of assets, of people, of industry, and of political power, and lead to the greatest sprawl that the region had yet seen.

The partial amalgamation established a regional government called Metropolitan Toronto that appropriated the thirteen jurisdiction's trunk sewers, water mains, sewage and water treatment, transit, and regional roads.[25] In effect, it merged one set of very valuable utilities – those of the city – with liability-ridden suburban utilities[26] whose ill-functioning facilities were in need of removal. One Toronto alderman, noting the lop-sided nature of the asset transfer, commented: 'We seem to be requested to give everything, and in return get nothing but possibly higher taxes.'[27]

Partial Amalgamation, Full Sprawl   61

The higher taxes, and higher utility rates, soon came, as Metro Toronto, headed by Gardiner, launched a massive program of public works, one unprecedented in scale and cost. Over the next fourteen years, it built one hundred miles of trunk sewers, constructed three new lake-based sewage treatment plants, and enlarged the capacity of a fourth.[28] Meanwhile, Metro Toronto closed most of the suburban municipalities' small-scale sewage treatment plants and connected their local sewers to the newly built trunk sewers. By the time this construction phase was over, in 1967, almost the entire population of Metropolitan Toronto was served by a modern lake-based sewer system.[29] The total cost of these sewage works was $100 million.

Simultaneously, Metro embarked on a massive waterworks program, expanding four water filtration plants, constructing a fifth and planning a sixth. It also constructed new reservoirs and built more than one hundred miles of trunk mains. These waterworks enabled Metro to close suburban well-water plants and provide treated lake water to all Metro residents. The total cost of these major drinking-water projects ran to another $100 million.[30]

A further $200 million went into road building. To improve traffic between municipalities, particularly in the suburban municipalities, Metro constructed new arterial roads, bridges, grade-separated railway crossings, and major intersections. Metro also built three major expressways – the Gardiner, the Don Valley, and the Allen – to enable suburbanites to commute to the city centre.

Metro spent massively in expanding public transit, too: Within a decade, the TTC's route mileage had increased by 75 per cent, mostly to accommodate suburbanites.[31] Building new schools also required great spending. Between 1954 and 1964, the public school enrolment in Metro increased by 92,700 pupils, 92 per cent of it in the suburbs.[32] All told, 'nearly the whole Metro program until now has been in or for the suburbs,'[34] Gardiner stated in 1958.[33]

The financing for this massive Metro program, although predominantly for the suburbs, came predominantly from the City of Toronto. Because Toronto had 62 per cent of Metro's tax base in 1954, it provided 62 per cent of the capital funding.[34] In effect, Metro was a redistribution machine that took taxes from the city in order to fund services needed in the suburbs. Indeed, this was its very purpose.[35] As Commissioner H. Carl Goldenberg, in his review of Metropolitan Toronto in 1965 put it: 'One of the main purposes for the creation of Metro was to pool the resources of the area for the provision of certain essential services of area-wide significance. In respect of education, such pooling necessarily means that the municipalities with larger resources, like Toronto, will contribute more in taxes than they receive from Metropolitan revenues.'[36] Without this pooling, the suburbs would not be able to finance their services. 'It has been estimated recently that it would require taxes derived from a house selling at approximately $27,000.00 for a municipality to break even, and for many this is just unrealistic,' a Metro Toronto planner reported.[37]

In some cases, such as in the provision of utility services, the *Metropolitan Toronto Act* required the utility to be financially self-sustaining, without reliance on property taxes. Here the subsidies came not from tax rolls but through the utility bills, which averaged the costs of supplying high- and low-cost customers.[38] In the case of water, Toronto residents were paying 8.72 cents per 1,000 gallons prior to Metro's creation.[39] By 1959, their water rate had almost doubled, to 16.87 cents. Residents in most suburbs, in contrast, saw their water rates decrease, in one case by 30 per cent. As a 1964 report prepared by the city stated: 'The progressively higher Metro charges have arisen essentially from severely greater charges incurred in expanding the supply of water to some suburbs. Had Metro not been formed, these costs would have fallen upon the suburban municipalities in question.'[40]

Likewise, the TTC subsidized uneconomic suburban riders at the fare box by departing from its pay-by-distance system, which required a greater fare from passengers travelling a greater distance. This costly change, which led to rapid increases in fares and, consequently, rapidly declining ridership,[41] came at the insistence of suburban councillors, who wanted to relieve their constituents of the full expense of commuting. In fact, all utility services, as well as taxes, were now determined by politicians intent on obtaining for their constituents maximum services at minimum cost.

To make matters worse for Toronto, its residents also saw their local tax burden increase as a byproduct of Metro's expressways, which worsened congestion within the city by bringing in more traffic than the city's roads were designed to handle. The added wear and tear shortened the life of city streets, requiring them to be prematurely repaired or rebuilt, and it led to a need for road widenings. 'With the growing number of suburban commuters and the steady rise in the ratio of motor vehicles to population, [Toronto] was faced with the need for extensive street improvements to relieve traffic congestion,' concluded Commissioner H. Carl Goldenberg in *Report of the Royal Com-*

mission on Metropolitan Toronto.[42] He was in agreement with the city, which had argued that 'the expensive metropolitan roadway improvements, of which the Gardiner Expressway stands first, are not beneficial to the central city.'[43] Even earlier, in 1952, Toronto Mayor Allan Lamport had opposed the funding of the Gardiner Expressway from taxes, proposing instead that it be privately built and financed by tolls.[44]

The Metro Toronto system of governance did not favour Toronto. Although Toronto had the majority of Metro's residents, it didn't have the majority of the votes on Metro council – the Metro chair, appointed by the province, could cast the deciding vote in all city-suburban splits, and he saw his duty as the development of the suburbs.[45] With Toronto politicians outvoted, city residents found themselves subsidizing the suburbs' development. Unrestrained by the need for fiscal discipline, suburban growth exploded. The suburban population soon reached that of the city and by 1967 had soared to 1.2 million.[46] Unlike the city's development, however, the new suburban growth was not compact, its density just half that of the city.[47]

With time, the suburbs' political clout magnified. As they grew in population, they sought, and got, more votes still on Metro council, tilting policies further toward suburban interests.[48] The city of Toronto, seeing its power wane, renewed its demand for a full amalgamation of the jurisdictions within Metro. In 1969, it held a referendum, in which 82 per cent voted for full amalgamation. Despite the convincing result, the province refused to redraw the city's boundaries.[49]

Had the province granted full amalgamation in 1969, little would have changed. By then the suburbs had become populated and would have represented a majority voting bloc in a fully amalgamated city council. Also by then, the city's institutions, and especially the TTC, had been transformed. No longer was the public transit system run by engineers who took pride in providing service where the numbers warranted; now it was run by politicians who placed routes where politically expedient.

Had the province granted a full amalgamation in 1950, in contrast, everything would have changed. The small numbers who would then have been living in the newly amalgamated areas would have been entitled to some improved services, at modest cost to other Toronto taxpayers. They would never have received 'almost the whole of the municipal budget,' to paraphrase Metro Chairman Gardiner. The sparsely populated lands of the new Toronto would have remained largely undeveloped for long periods of time.[52] These areas had few votes on city council and would have had no ability to impose their will on the tax-paying majority.

The 1969 referendum drew a curtain in Toronto's making. Its suburbs were mostly developed; the wasteful investments in infrastructure were mostly completed, and Metro's population growth had slowed to a crawl.[51] Rapid growth was, however, occurring in the adjacent municipalities. The population of Mississauga, to the west of Metro, doubled between 1971 and 1981, and the population of Markham, to the north, rose 37 per cent in the five years between 1976 and 1981.[52] A new round of sprawl was well underway.

8 The Suburbs beyond the Suburbs

WITH SATISH DHAR

The province's creation of Metropolitan Toronto accomplished its goals. Through this partial amalgamation mechanism, the suburbs were financed and methodically filled in.

But partial amalgamation was not the province's only financing mechanism in the years following the Second World War. The province also spawned suburban expansion through infrastructure projects that would mesh Toronto with its immediate suburbs and beyond. These flowed from far-reaching plans begun by prewar planning bodies.

As the end of the war neared, political leaders established planning agencies to provide for the betterment of the people. The City Planning Board, created as Toronto's first official planning board in 1942, by 1943 had produced a thirty-year master plan that called for vast slum clearances and superhighways. By 1945, the city had begun Regent Park, Canada's first large public housing project. In 1946 the province brought in a planning act to encourage municipalities to develop official plans for their communities.

The planning anticipated, and relished, a postwar population boom that would settle the countryside. At a 1944 municipal conference on planning and development attended by hundreds of municipal delegates, Premier George Drew exhorted his audience to 'go to the limits of the imagination' in expanding the population, stating that there was 'no reason why this province cannot maintain 25 million in a higher degree of prosperity than ever before.' The province soon did go to the limit, reconstructing itself as a lower-density land. The creation of Metropolitan Toronto, funded by city taxpayers and ratepayers, was phase one in the dispersion of the population. Phase two took in Metro and beyond. It would be funded by the province.

Highway 401, now among the world's busiest freeways, was initially designed in the late 1940s to be a low-volume, trans-provincial highway well north of Toronto,[1] its 'Toronto Bypass' specifically intended for through traffic only. Completed in 1956, the twenty-six-mile bypass ran through the undeveloped outer suburbs of Scarborough, North York and Etobicoke. It was a motorist's dream, according to one Toronto newspaper, providing 'some of the most soothing scenery in the Metropolitan area ... It winds smoothly through pastures and across streams and rivers, and beside green thickets. It seems a long way from the big city.'

The 'bypass' role of the twenty-six-mile stretch soon changed, and the highway soon stopped seeming a long way from the city. In line with the province's decision to amalgamate Toronto's metropolitan area, and with federal efforts to develop Toronto's suburbs, the province constructed interchanges at every major intersection along the length of the bypass. Dormitory communities then sprang up in the northern fringe of the Toronto area and beyond as the Highway 401 bypass became a predominantly short-trip, commuter highway. By 1959, a highway that but three years earlier was estimated to carry 48,000 cars per day was now carrying 185,000 cars per day, and rush-hour traffic jams had routinely reduced highway speeds to fifteen miles per hour. To the 401's original two lanes in each direction, the provincial government then added three collector lanes in each direction, to handle local traffic. By 1962 construction had begun and the 401 had become a twelve-lane freeway. In addition to building Highway 401, the province built or widened other highways to service the suburbs northwest, north, and northeast of Metro.[2] None of the costs associated with any of these highways was borne by the local communities that relied upon them.

In another step to make the suburbs viable, the province in 1967 began a commuter rail system, GO Transit, that expanded over the next 20 years from an initial 90-mile corridor to a 900-mile network of bus and rail. Because demand from passengers could not justify GO Transit, the province paid for the entire capital costs, and much of the operating cost, too. In 1978, eleven years after it began operations, the province provided GO Transit system with 42 per cent of its operating budget and in 1992, with 38 per cent, making the subsidy per passenger $2.30 out of an average fare of $5.21.[3]

The province also decided to build water and sewage systems outside Metro Toronto through the Ontario Water Resources Commission, an agency it created in 1956. This agency first provided water and sewage capacity to municipalities west of Metro Toronto, particularly the fast growing communities of Brampton and Mississauga,[4] and then negotiated with municipalities to the north (Richmond Hill, Markham, Aurora, and Newmarket) and east of Metro (Pickering and Ajax) to build a costly water and trunk sewer system called York-Durham.[5]

Even so, the suburban communities were struggling. 'In many areas, the existing local governments are not able to cope with the speed and the magnitude of the challenges that face them – challenges that involve population growth, changing patterns of urban and suburban areas, huge and expensive problems of providing water lines and sewers, traffic jams so severe that they have a serious impact on the economy and so on,' stated Darcy McKeough, the minister of municipal affairs. The Ontario government viewed the municipal growth as an urgent problem needing drastic reform, 'nothing less than a complete overhaul of the municipal system – the most dramatic and far-reaching series of changes in 120 years,' McKeough stated. 'Our municipalities are facing a large-scale, long-term crises. To meet this, they need large-scale, long-term solutions.'[6]

The dizzying pace of change in the 1960s, and its cost, also alarmed Ontario's premier, John Robarts, who saw municipal reform as the challenge for the 1970s. Toronto was especially a problem child. By the late 1960s, the 'hippie threat' in the Yorkville district had become a cause célèbre, the target of crusading politicians. The Toronto Board of Control, concerned about Yorkville's 'overcrowded living quarters,' sent extra policemen to the district. Controller Allan Lamport, calling Yorkville a 'blot on the city,' tried to establish an 8 pm curfew. Police chief Mackay argued that Sunday school should be made compulsory to deal with youth's attitudes towards marijuana, LSD, the sexual revolution, civil disobedience over the Vietnam War, and other matters that he feared were causing a 'world-wide moral breakdown.' South of the border, the highly publicized President's Crime Commission linked drugs and organized crime, leading Toronto police to link Yorkville hippies with organized crime and harass them with vagrancy charges and Yorkville coffee houses with licensing requirements. Accusations of police brutality added to the area's reputation for disorder.[7]

To cope with this unsettling social change and maintain the province's standard of living, Premier John Robarts decided it would be necessary for government to curb people's freedoms. As he explained in 1970, the individual 'is inevitably going to be subjected to more controls for the benefit of all.'

There will be greater controls in the use of land. There will be controls, in my opinion, that our people are not necessarily used to. I want them to understand why we are doing it. If we are to do what must be done to avoid the enormous urban problems of our neighbours in the United States, governments will have to step in and say 'Thou shalt not.' If they say that, they are going to have the understanding and the agreement of the people to whom they are speaking because we cannot do it in a vacuum. It can only be done if people really understand that it is not for the government that we are doing these things; it is for the people who ask us to look after their total interest.

Robarts made his plea for public understanding in unveiling a development plan for the Toronto region. He was chiefly describing the need to control where people live:

For several years we have been working in the province to create a program of regional economic planning and development. This is going to bring some large changes in thinking by our people and by our governments. For instance, we want the better dispersion of people throughout the ten economic regions into which we have divided Ontario. We are not going to be able to allow people just to go where they want, because this may create many problems. We need planning to make sure that we make better economic use of our resources. We will be calling for more orderly land planning and use of land; of course, as always, there will be difficulties in this area ... we started dealing with transportation but we found we could not deal with transportation in isolation. We were automatically led into total examination and total planning for the whole area.

Within a month, Robarts explained, he would be unveiling Design for Development: Toronto-Centred Region,[8] 'which encompasses a 90-mile arc around Metropolitan Toronto ... We started with this area because it probably is the area which most needs some type of control.'

I am sure you will all agree that the question of the eventual size of Metropolitan Toronto cannot be treated as a separate question apart from all the rest of the province and particularly the orderly development of the central part of the province.

We are concerned. Our plans are designed to assist us in dealing with the problems of congestion, transportation, pollution, balanced economic growth and the quality of life, and by this we mean green spaces and open air, fresh air parks, access to water, fishing and shooting, skiing and camping, and all the things that people want to do. That is the quality of life which is so very important in the years ahead. None of these things can be done in isolation. Therefore we are going to have to have co-ordinated planning unprecedented in our history ... Eventually it will lead to the adoption and implementation of a total provincial planning policy.[9]

Low-density developments were prohibitively expensive to finance. And yet high-density urban developments, Robarts feared, brought with them unwanted social ills. Metro had been created to deal with an overpopulated City of Toronto whose residents then spilled out to the outskirts, causing upheaval, many in government circles believed.[10] Robarts did not want a repeat of the uncontrolled growth that Toronto's suburbs had seen. His solution was to limit growth just outside Metro through a giant arc of greenbelt that would remain, apart from existing communities, mostly rural. Beyond the greenbelt, however, the region's rural character would diminish: the greenbelt would channel growth to more distant communities, increasing their density and thus the efficiency at which services could be delivered to them.

And to finance all this, Robarts decided to repeat the partial amalgamation approach that had financed the city of Toronto's immediate suburbs.[11] In the same way that the province had created Metropolitan Toronto to take responsibility for Metro-wide services, the province now created four regional municipalities in what would become known as the Greater Toronto Area.[12] The cost of regional services provided by these regional municipalities would be funded by local municipalities that pooled their taxes on the basis of the assessed value of the properties in their jurisdictions.[13]

But what worked so well in supporting Toronto's immediate suburbs fell short in the suburbs outside Metro. The local communities were too poor to finance their regional services on the basis of pooled taxes alone – these communities had developed as fringe dormitory extensions of Toronto, at lower population densities than those found in the Metro Toronto suburbs. Moreover, apart from Mississauga, no local community dominated its region either in population size or in fiscal wealth, leaving no rich assessment base to share across a region.[14] The local communities thus became lobbyists for provincial relief, those within the greenbelt also seeking relief from greenbelt limitations.

By now these communities, creations of government policies, represented potent voting blocs. The province, fearing electoral defeat, conceded.[15] The cash flowed and the much-vaunted greenbelt, over time, was whittled down to a utility corridor that today hosts, among other facilities, the new Highway 407. Other attempts to control uneconomic suburban growth through planning – over the last three decades Ontario has had a never ending procession of regional plans, official acts, policy statements, planning boards, task forces and programs – met similar fates.[16]

Because the province was determined to limit the population of Metropolitan Toronto and better disperse the provincial population through regional municipalities, it had few options. The funding predicament could be seen in the case of the public school system, which accounted for the lion's share of local government budgets. In 1975, for example, public schools constituted 52 per cent of all local government outlays outside Metro,[17] a figure that would grow even larger.[18] Because the rural municipalities could not afford to provide a public school education for the families they were attracting, the province, again, provided grants.[19]

Likewise, in setting up the regional municipalities, the province had hoped that they would fund infrastructure projects such as the York-Durham pipeline project. This was not to be. Because York and Durham were not viable financially for infrastructure on this scale, the provincial government, and to a lesser extent the federal government, ultimately subsidized this project, which took nine years and $297 million to complete. For the regional municipalities, it was a bargain. User fees financed only $69 million, or about 23 per cent.

Because of such bargains, bargain-hunters, in the form of new suburban residents, presented themselves in large numbers. Upon the pipeline's completion in 1984, the local communities along the pipeline became the fastest-growing urban areas in their regions. But their gain occurred at the cost of Metro and especially the City of Toronto. Between 1971 and 1976, Metro Toronto's population had stagnated and that of the City of Toronto had shrunk by 11 per cent. In contrast, the number of people living in the four regions had swelled by 25 per cent.[20]

Speaking at a 1982 conference, June Rowlands, a City of Toronto councillor who would later become mayor, criticized the province's lavish funding of new communities that were drawing away Toronto residents. 'Metro has infrastructure in place to sustain a population of 3 million people,' she stated, enough to accommodate an additional population of 860,000 people. 'At the provincial level there are two policies that are seriously affecting Metropolitan Toronto's ability to retain its population. First, there is the Big Pipe [the York-Durham pipeline] adjacent to Metro boundaries and second, there are very large provincial subsidies that are funding expressways, super highways and especially GO Transit.'[21]

In effect, City of Toronto residents subsidized the costs of the Metro suburbs through levies of various kinds and Metro residents subsidized the costs of the outer Greater Toronto Area suburbs through their provincial taxes. As a result, subsidies in the Greater Toronto Area flowed outwards in concentric ripples from the more dense, more developed communities toward the more thinly built-up suburbs.[22]

Those concentric ripples, in turn, also reflect the level of sprawl. Today, the population density of that central city – the City of Toronto with its pre-1998 amalgamation boundaries – is twenty-eight people per acre.[23] The densities of Toronto's three outer suburbs, North York, Etobicoke and Scarborough, range from ten to thirteen people per acre.[24] Beyond these three outer suburbs lie the communities within the four regional municipalities of Halton, Peel, York, and Durham: These communities' densities range from six to eight people per acre. The central city, in other words, is more than twice as dense as its immediate suburbs and four times as dense as its outermost suburbs.[25]

Toronto's suburbs have sprawled in inverse relationship to the subsidies they received, and for a self-evident reason: Many if not most of the developments that occurred outside Toronto were uneconomic, and would not have occurred without subsidy. This is how Toronto sprawled.

Conclusion: How Toronto Might Have Been

Through subsidies and prohibitions, governments succeeded in dispersing Toronto's population. As a result, the Greater Toronto Area developed in concentric arcs around the centre city that was Toronto, uniformly and at gradually decreasing densities as the distance from Toronto increased. The sharp division between urban and rural societies was thus blurred, and by design. As explained by Darcy McKeough, the minster of municipal affairs who, as much as anyone, changed the postwar landscape of the Toronto region: 'we could not accept the recommendations [that] called for a distinct separation of the area [west of Toronto] into two regions – one rural and one urban. Our view is that the division of urban and rural economies is a method of the past.'[1] So it was. By government decree. Rather than have high population, compact communities abutting rural regions sprinkled with towns, the government homogenized the Greater Toronto Area to make it more of a soup. Urban densities were reduced, and rural densities raised, giving much of both a suburban quality. We thus lost the traditional character of both city and rural lands.

The government decree in the Toronto of the 1970s, like the government decrees in earlier decades of the century, were often justified on economic grounds but were, in fact, entirely uneconomic, the product of well-meaning reformers and the politicians that shared their visions. The public's preferences, overwhelmingly and over time, lay elsewhere. Starting in the last half of the nineteenth century and continuing well into the twentieth, Canadians in large number were leaving rural areas for Toronto and other cities. After each world war, returning servicemen determined to live in Toronto and other cities, and during the Second World War, too, although the government banned such migration.

Immigrants to Canada through most of its history overwhelmingly settled in cities. In all these cases, while individuals sought to dwell in cities, governments sought to thwart their desires.

Popular mythology has people flocking to North America's idyllic new suburbs after Second World War out of a natural desire for more land and a safer environment in which to raise their children, and that governments were only facilitating a public clamouring for a suburban lifestyle. Government planners believe this, too.[2] Yet the definitive study of that period in Toronto's history, *The Suburban Society* by University of Toronto sociologist S.D. Clark, demonstrates through detailed surveys that few chose the suburbs to escape the city, to be closer to nature, or to find surroundings more conducive to raising children. Just as in previous eras, those who chose to live on the city's periphery did so to acquire cheaper housing, not a superior lifestyle. Of these, most moved half-heartedly.

'People were forced into the suburbs in search of living space,' Clark states in his 1966 book, explaining the choice in terms of passivism and resignation. 'It was, by and large, those people the least reluctant to abandon residence in the city who made the move to the suburbs. To this extent, in the populating of the suburbs, there were selective forces at work. The suburban population had about it a negative quality at least ... the people who moved to the suburbs were largely indifferent about where they lived.'

As seen in Clark's surveys, most people knew little about the lifestyle that awaited them in the suburbs and, in one survey, 'very few indicated having made any effort to learn about the area in which they were buying a house. "I was green – we got this place in a week," ... "We didn't know too much about the district – we just came up and when we saw the houses it was nothing but mud," "We bought this house from ads in paper – a real estate man brought us out – we looked at it and we signed the papers within one day if not the same day," were the ways some of the residents described embarking upon a career of home-ownership.'

At the end of the Second World War, the hinterlands that were Toronto's suburbs held few attractions apart from cost savings. Suburban settlements then tended to be on inconveniently situated land ill-suited for farming, and thus available at low cost. Clark described the prospects facing one lower-middle class suburban community that established itself north of Toronto in the mid-1950s along and back of Bayview, which was then an uncleared right-of-way:

It was to be a bitter discovery on the part of these people just how exceedingly inadequate were the public services in the area and how impossible it was to secure improvement except at exorbitant cost. A small group of residents could not by themselves build up and support the kind of community services required and, so long as these sorts of services were not available, there was not likely to be any increase in the number of residents. What had been created was a little residential pocket, almost idyllic in superficial appearances, but doomed to be deprived for a long time to come of much that was essential to the existence of an urban residential community.

The obstacles to the establishment of middle-class residential settlements in the country by the movement out from the city of individual families on their own were almost insuperable and not many such settlements came into being. Where the movement, however, was of a population which had little concern about the quality of public services, there was virtually no limit to the development which could take place in areas where land had little value for any purpose other than residential use.

Thus it was that the taking over of the countryside in this early phase of movement of population from the city was most successfully accomplished by people in impoverished circumstances prepared to accept whatever the country had to offer them in preference to what was available to them in the city.[3]

Historian Patricia Hart in *Pioneering in North York* likewise describes the absence of amenity in the most populous of Toronto's suburbs, in the years immediately before and after the war:

Ratepayer Associations were soon formed in each district to take up the cry for water, the spraying of mosquitoes, roads, and better bus service. In order to consolidate their efforts a Central Community Council was established on September 7, 1945, to coordinate all district organizations interested in promoting social, cultural, recreational, and educational activities in the Township. Up to this time communities had no shopping facilities, bus service was infrequent, and there was no entertainment or recreational facilities. People borrowed from their neighbours, and there was much visiting back and forth ...

Most roads to the city were still only two lanes wide. One of the few exceptions was Yonge Street, and the two-lane bridge on it was an effective bottleneck. Side streets were often covered with cinders, but by 1947 builders had to provide gravel roads in new subdivisions.

The absence of amenities, and the prohibitive cost that would have been required to make most suburban communities attractive, largely limited their expansion to the poor. A 1951 survey of Scarborough dwellings reveals that only 72 per cent had flush toilets, 57 per cent had gas or electric refrigerators, 77 per cent had furnaces and 63 per cent had telephones. Other suburbs in the Toronto area differed little. Suburbs were popularly referred to in uncomplimentary fashion, through generic terms such as 'the burbs' and 'the sticks,' and specific ones such as 'Scarberia' in the case of Scarborough. Suburban dwellers likewise lacked status, in some cases strikingly so. *Pioneering in North York* described the 'cave dwellers' of North York, as Toronto newspapers called them: 'They dug basements, covered them over, then paused to regroup their finances, and as the idea became known, others followed suit. They were somewhat derisively called "cave dwellers." Slowly, these houses have been finished, sometimes after a nudge from the municipal authorities, but for a number of years 'cave dwellers' walked daily to a pump near the centre of the community for water.'[4]

Even the prize-winning and ultimately successful North York district of Don Mills, which epitomizes the postwar suburban ideal of a planned community, has a reputation born of revisionist history: Although popular with planners, with the populace at large it was anything but. 'It is hard to believe, but Don Mills was something to scoff at when it was first conceived,' writes Hart. 'Everyone on North York Council was opposed, with the exception of Reeve McMahon. Mortgage money was difficult to get because the lending companies could not visualize it ... House buyers, used to the old style boxes, were reluctant to accept the more imaginative architecture of Don Mills.'[5] Don Mills, in any case, was not completed until 1960. By then, government had created the suburban dream.

It took a concerted effort on the part of governments to change the landscape enough to make suburban living thinkable for the broad middle class. 'Indeed, it is scarcely possible to escape the feeling that there was something almost fraudulent about the whole vast enterprise directed to the object of persuading people to move to the suburbs,' Clark concluded. Because the suburbs' initial appeal could only lay in price, government assumed the risks, provided the infrastructure, offered grants and subsidies, and otherwise set out to create the conditions necessary to lower housing costs in the suburbs enough to make it competitive with urban residence. Had government not delivered on price, there is no reason to believe that the public's postwar lifestyle preference would have differed from that preceding the war, and that of earlier generations, too.[6]

Governments had many reasons for diverting people from cities, most of them well-intentioned.[7] One reason stands above all, however, especially over the course of the twentieth century: Politicians saw the change in cities, ever the hothouse for social innovations, as destabilizing.[8] To dampen this change, they manipulated the levers of the economy – taxes, fees grants, regulations – to steer settlement away from cities to more placid settings. Had they not done so, and instead allowed the social forces to play out, Toronto and other major cities would have evolved much differently.

Without fear that urban life was conducive to socialists and union organizing, and inconducive to creating men and women of good moral fibre, governments would not have crafted programs during both world wars to house returning servicemen outside cities. They would not have devised public health programs to evict the city's poor from downtowns. They would not have banned, throughout most of Toronto, apartment buildings and other housing geared to single people. They would not have thwarted the practice of families taking in boarders, and of families sharing houses. They would not have treated immigrants as threats to the social order. Or cleared entire city blocks of compact housing in now-prized areas such as Cabbagetown to build public housing such as the now-derelict Regent Park.[9] Or converted prime agricultural lands to sprawling suburb, to house those who might otherwise reside inside cities.

Without such government policies, Toronto's existing buildings and neighbourhoods would have remained compact and intact, to be upgraded and adapted by their owners and occupants as new needs presented themselves; Toronto's new buildings and neighbourhoods would likewise have been built compactly, as was then the style and custom of Toronto and other cities in North America and Europe. That era, which preceded formal government planning, gave us the older districts that most today consider the handsome portion of our cities. More of Toronto would have been handsome.

More of its suburbs would been, too. Before the era of subsidized sprawl, suburbs developed compactly, along transportation corridors. Some were elegant or valued for their amenities, such as the Beaches, originally a resort area for Toronto; others, such as the Junction Triangle, were working-class suburbs, built around factories located outside cities to serve city markets. Beyond these compact suburbs, still a short distance from the transportation corridor, lay farmland, again serving urban markets.

But even these compact suburbs would have been fewer in number, and slower to materialize, than those which we now have. When the government did not backstop private developers, as was more the case in the first half of the twentieth century, the private sector was leery of prematurely developing land or transit routes. It tended to wait until the population was substantial enough to warrant expansion, rather than espouse a 'build it and they will come' philosophy. Too often, developers had recklessly 'built it' and they did not come, and the developers had become bankrupts.

This caution among private entrepreneurs served to make Toronto stable: Because the city's private transit company did not open up the suburbs early in the twentieth century, as its U.S. counterparts often did, Toronto's middle class made neighbourhoods such as the Annex and High Park their home, creating an attractive housing stock within the city too valuable to later be lightly abandoned.[10] Only after the government nationalized the transit utility, and profits became less important to the utility than expansion, could Toronto's suburban communities compete with city neighbourhoods for the regard of the middle class. Even so, and even with the uneconomic roads to the suburbs that Metro and the province built, Toronto has retained its middle-class neighbourhoods, countering the stereotype of the city as a place for the very rich and very poor.

The city of Toronto that governments aborted when they created a metropolitan government in the 1950s could have comfortably housed most of the population that subsequently would move to its suburbs, and also most of the population that would subsequently move to the suburbs beyond. At about the population density of New York's Greenwich Village, for example, the city of Toronto could have housed Metro's entire population of today. At about the population density of New York's West Side and Upper West Side, the city of Toronto could also have housed most of the balance of what is now known as the Greater Toronto Area.[11] Toronto could have been as compact as desirable areas of New York, or of Paris, Milan, and other attractive European cities.

Had governments not aborted the dense city that could have been Toronto's destiny, there would have been no rationale for the partial amalgamation that created Metro in the 1950s, or for the regional governments that came in the 1970s, or for the full amalgamation that came in the 1990s, or for the Greater Toronto agencies touted for the 2000s. Aside from the suburbs hugging transportation routes, these areas would have remained Toronto's hinterlands, mostly as agricultural lands, towns and villages attached.

Postscript: Toronto in 2020

In all likelihood, Toronto will continue to sprawl. This has been its history, a history that is already repeating itself. The Greater Toronto Area is gaining the status of a political jurisdiction, with region-wide bodies touted as the answer to the region's disarray and inefficiency. A formal GTA authority, first to run transit, then to assume responsibility for water and sewerage, roads, garbage, and policing would surprise no one. And after the region was partially amalgamated in this way, a full amalgamation would be a logical next step.[1]

Yet there are also plausible prospects for a slowdown in sprawl and, less plausibly, for an absolute halt to sprawl, perhaps even a reversal. New reforms that are on the horizon, although designed for other purposes, would inadvertently be sprawl stoppers. Their implementation could come by 2020.

The congestion pricing of roads. Since London reduced traffic congestion in its downtown core by tolling private vehicles at peak hours, some one hundred cities around the world have indicated an interest in controlling road use. More concretely, the government of the European Union, and of the United Kingdom in particular, have universal road tolling as formal policy.[2] Under the scheme that they envision, all private vehicles would be tracked by satellite or other electronic technology, and billed for their use of roads, based on the type of road, the level of its congestion, environmental factors, and other criteria. If jurisdictions implement road tolling as planned over the 2015–20 period, private automobiles and trucks would face per-mile charges to cover the costs of road use, with fees rising dramatically during times of congestion.

The distance-based component of the tolls – a relatively small fee – would only modestly discourage commuting if Toronto adopted road tolling. The congestion component of the tolls, which would especially affect rush-hour travel, would have much more dramatic effect. While no studies exist for the Toronto area, studies for other jurisdictions often put the cost of rush-hour commuter travel well above $1 per mile travelled.[3] A fifty-mile one-way peak-hour commute, in other words, could cost a prohibitive $100 per day, reversing any savings that may have persuaded someone to purchase a house in the suburbs rather than in the city. With such pricing, many would change their residence or place of work to shorten travel distances, relieving congestion on roads and eliminating the demand for new roads. Without new roads, low-density sprawl would all but halt.

Replacing market value assessment with user fees. Taxation of property in Ontario is based on its value, through a system known as market value assessment. This system taxes most highly the properties in the downtown Toronto core, both commercial and residential. In effect, the property tax acts as a tax on density, punishing the land that is most highly prized, and thus has the highest real estate value. Land less in demand, generally land distant from Toronto's downtown, has a lower market value and thus is taxed less. The market value system of taxation is all the more perverse given differences in the cost of delivering services: Because lots in low-density areas tend to have larger frontages, these lots require more sidewalk, more road, more gas, water and sewer pipeline, and more electricity line to service. Likewise, because the distances between houses is larger in low-density areas, garbage trucks can make fewer pickups in a day, fire stations can cover fewer houses within their service area, public transit vehicles can collect fewer passengers within the catchment area of their route.

Were taxes based on market value assessment replaced by user fees on municipal utility services, so that these services fully recovered their own cost, sprawl would likely stop. Not only would the tax on density have ended, removing the penalty that people have paid to work and live in high-value areas, but so would the subsidy to low-density areas. With suburbs raising rates to cover services such as water and electricity distribution, which have high fixed costs, and cutting back on services with high operating costs, such as public transit and garbage collection, fewer people would opt to establish their homes and businesses in low-density surroundings.[1]

While the complete replacement of market value assessment with user fees is unlikely, a partial replacement is not: jurisdictions throughout the developed world are privatizing municipal services or reducing subsidies in such areas as public transit, power production, water and sewerage and garbage collection. Any move toward market pricing in any of these areas would act to discourage sprawl.

Replacing market value assessment with other forms of taxation. More benign forms of taxation than market value assessment would also reduce sprawl. Many cities raise revenue through municipal income taxes, sales taxes, or gas taxes.[5] Should Toronto become such a city, as it has been demanding, the bias against high-value properties would diminish and, to the extent that these taxes displace market value property taxes, sprawl would be ameliorated.

This change in tax collection would have a minimal affect on the affluent, who would still live centrally, and still pay a disproportionate share of taxes through progressive income taxes, rather than through high property taxes. The middle class, for whom living costs loom large in determining living location, would be greatly affected.[6] In the 1980 to 2000 period, some 10 per cent of Toronto's middle class abandoned the city. Many of those who left cities for suburbs on economic grounds would return; many of those who would in future be leaving due to living costs would stay. These changes would bolster Toronto's tax base but deprive some suburbs of an important proportion of their tax base, nudging them toward the suburbs' former role as downscale, working-class districts able to provide their residents little beyond basic services.[7]

Widespread deregulation. Much less plausible still than these scenarios is a sea-change away from central planning, leading to widespread deregulation, not only in terms of privatizing municipal utilities but also in abandoning zoning and other restrictions that now prohibit dense developments in cities and suburbs alike. Through such laws, people are forbidden to live in some districts and businesses are forbidden to operate in others, forcing commutes on people who would otherwise be living and working in the same district.[8]

The single-most object of regulation, the automobile, has produced the single biggest cause of sprawl and the single biggest deterrent to compact cities. To accommodate the automobile, planners require an inordinate amount of road space, almost all of it subsidized.

Such government requirements are often done in the name of limiting the auto. To allay neighbourhood concerns about vehicles parking on side streets, for example, Toronto forces developers to provide excess on-site parking, even for apartment buildings located at subway stops, and catering to transit users. As a result, Toronto has a large government-driven oversupply of parking spots: building managers report that as many as half the underground spots on offer remain unoccupied, even though building owners often lease the spots to the general public. Such surplus parking both lowers the cost of driving in Toronto and inflates the cost of city living. The construction costs for underground parking in Toronto ranges from $25,000 to $30,000 per space, equivalent, in some cases, to the land cost per unit. These costs are passed on to apartment dwellers.[9]

Myriad other regulations also discriminate against high-density developments. They include requirements that apartments include kitchens, which needlessly raise the cost of downtown living for those who prefer to frequent neighbourhood restaurants for their meals (such apartments were once common) and onerous height and density restrictions. Along major thoroughfares such as the downtown stretch of Bloor, served by both subway and streetcar lines, for example, buildings are limited to 16 metres in height and the equivalent of three floors of either office or residential units. The city even prescribes what portion of the three-storey limit can be office and what portion residential. In other instances, the city imposes densities that effectively limit the square footage of buildings to one-fifth the area of the lot.[10]

While zoning regulations doubtless benefit some residents, for the vast majority of city residents these regulations represent only costs. They are, in effect, hidden levies that deter city living. Should widespread deregulation end such regulations, not only would future sprawl stop, past sprawl would be reversed.

As the postwar suburbs have aged, many have been abandoned by the middle class for new suburbs farther out. Into these decaying suburbs have moved immigrants seeking cheaper housing. With remote suburbs costly and services poor, the middle class would in future abandon the aging postwar suburbs for locations farther in. And poor immigrants, rather than occupying these aging suburbs for their inexpensive housing, would more often prefer city locations, to avoid transportation expenses.

Should these aging suburbs be abandoned by residential users, some would revert over time to farmland, to meet the immense demand by

Toronto restaurants, grocers, landscapers, and others for niche agricultural products, and especially for fresh produce – as it is, the GTA's agricultural output far surpasses that of any of the Maritime provinces.[11]

Under a full deregulation that encompassed immigration, however, few existing suburban districts would contract. New immigrants, if allowed to settle where they choose, would chiefly come to the same major metropolitan areas that so many of their fellow countrymen had settled, to find friends and mates, familiar foods and customary dress, religious and social organizations. Overwhelmingly, the immigrants would come to Toronto, by many measures the world's most multicultural city. Toronto would then grow inward and upward, rather than outward.

Notes

Introduction

1 W.F. Maclean, MP, in ' A Greater Toronto,' address to the Empire Club of Canada, 7 November 1907 (Toronto: The Empire Club of Canada, 1910).
2 Quoted in Christopher Armstrong and H.V. Nelles, *Monopoly's Moment: The Organization and Regulation of Canadian Utilities, 1830–1930* (Toronto: University of Toronto Press, 1986), p. 145.
3 After William Mackenzie's attempt in 1903 to have his Toronto and Hamilton Railroad Company granted a federal charter, provinces became alarmed at their loss of jurisdiction and joined forces with the Union of Canadian Municipalities. Future monopolies that governments granted generally gave muncipalities the right to regulate users of municipal streets.
4 Torontonians relied primarily upon well water. One study of Toronto in 1886, when the city's population was 120,000, reported 28,000 private wells. See John Mitchell, *The Settlement of York County* (Toronto: The Municipal Corporation of the County of York, 1950), p. 102.
5 In 1843 the Toronto Gas Light and Water Company began pumping water uphill from Lake Ontario by iron pipe. Service from this new and expensive technology was poor, very limited, and unpopular, leading to rancour, alternate suppliers, and ultimately a municipal takeover in 1872. The water service expanded under municipal ownership but became a laughing-stock because of frequent breakdowns and dirty tap water, and so onerous financially that the city debated a return of private waterworks into the late 1890s. See Armstrong and Nelles, *Monopoly's Moment*, pp. 13–20.
6 Maclean, 'A Greater Toronto.'
7 C.S. Clark, *Of Toronto the Good: The Queen City of Canada as It Is* (Montreal: The Toronto Publishing Company, 1898).

8 Timothy J. Colton, *Big Daddy: Frederick G. Gardiner and the Building of Metropolitan Toronto* (Toronto: University of Toronto Press, 1980), p. 21. Spadina Heights was self-governing as a public school section but otherwise not a legal jurisdiction. The Spadina Heights Residents' Association, desiring municipal services, petitioned the city for amalgamation and, when refused, it became incorporated as the Village of Forest Hill in 1923.
9 Frederick G. Gardiner, chairman of the Municipality of Metropolitan Toronto, in 'Metropolitan Toronto,' address to the Empire Club of Canada, 5 November 1953 (Toronto: The Empire Club Foundation, 1954).
10 York and East York Townships sought annexation in 1931. See Leslie H. Saunders, controller, in 'Amalgamation vs. Cumming Plan,' address to the Empire Club of Canada, 25 February 1953 (Toronto: The Empire Club Foundation, 1953). Forest Hill and Swansea were two exceptions.
11 The City of Toronto applied to the Ontario Municipal Board for an amalgamation of eleven municipalities and parts of two others.
12 Gardiner, 'Metropolitan Toronto.'

1. How Private Transit Hobbled Sprawl

1 W.F. Maclean, MP, in 'A Greater Toronto,' an address to the Empire Club of Canada, 7 November 1907 (Toronto: The Empire Club of Canada, 1910).
2 The Guild, formed in 1897, espoused the City Beautiful movement. Its 1909 plan also called for a system of parks and playgrounds, the development of the waterfront, and the beautification of city streets.
3 William Houston, 'The Evolution of a Greater Toronto,' an address to the Empire Club of Canada, 28 April 1910 (Toronto: The Empire Club of Canada, 1910). Houston also saw in his scheme an opportunity to widen existing roads and create new ones, in aid of developing the city's outskirts: 'Authority should be vested in some corporate body to control the laying out of streets in new territory and to correct defects in their lay-out in the old area of the city ... Two diagonal streets, one north-easterly and the other north-westerly should be laid out, of ample width, so as to save distance in reaching the centre of the city from the outskirts. This would give from the centre five ideal lines: Queen St. East, Queen St. West, Yonge St. North, and two diagonals.' Thomas Adams, among the most influential planners of his day, also sought wide roads, arguing that main thoroughfares be 100 feet wide, or 50 per cent wider than the 66-foot standard. See 'Present Scope for Practical Work in Improving Civic Conditions, 1916,' Conference of Civic Improvement League of Canada, held in cooperation with the Commission of Conservation, House of Commons, Ottawa, 10 January 1916.

4 Richard Harris, *Unplanned Suburbs: Toronto's American Tragedy, 1900 to 1950* (Baltimore: Johns Hopkins University Press, 1996), pp. 35–6.
5 The Metropolitan Street Railway Company of Toronto, which began service in 1885, would struggle and eventually be taken over by the Toronto & York Radial Railway Company, a subsidiary of Toronto Railway Company. Similarly, the Toronto and Mimico Electric Railway and Light Company, which began service in 1892, suspended service later that year. Other transit systems that had a short existence before abandoning service or being taken over included the Toronto and Scarboro' Electric Railway, Light and Power Company, the City and Suburban Electric Railway Company, the Davenport Street Railway Company, and Kingston Road Tramways Company.
6 Christopher Armstrong and H.V. Nelles, *Monopoly's Moment: The Organization and Regulation of Canadian Utilities, 1830–1930* (Toronto: University of Toronto Press, 1986), pp. 130–31. Porteous was William Mackenzie's business manager.
7 Many reformers, of course, wanted no private companies at all. The most prominent of these was Adam Beck, the visionary chairman of the Ontario Hydro-Electric Commission. Touting a Greater Hydro that would run transit as well as power systems, he intervened on numerous occasions to foil prospects for private transit utilities. See John R. Baldwin, *Regulatory Failure and Renewal: The Evolution of the Natural Monopoly Contract* (Ottawa: Economic Council of Canada, 1989).
8 Harris, *Unplanned Suburbs*, pp. 38–9. In important ways, Toronto's density was not comparable to New York's. New York covered a much larger area, including large tracts of undeveloped land, and Manhattan, its largest built-up area, had a very high density. Toronto had less undeveloped land, and a less-dense built-up area.
9 Toronto's population rose from 522,000 in the 1921 census to 631,000 in 1931 and 377,000 in 1911. Its suburbs grew from 33,000 in 1911 to 90,000 in 1921 and 187,000 in 1931.
10 The Toronto Railway Company's annual rate of return from 1900 to 1920 was 10 per cent. A study of U.S. transit companies for the period from 1909 to 1917 found that they earned 2.8 per cent.
11 Baldwin, *Regulatory Failure and Renewal*. The need to finance suburban lines did not account for the entire rate increase. Because of inflation during the First World War, the Toronto Railway Company's rates had become inadequate.
12 H.W. Tate, assistant general manager, Toronto Transportation Commission, in 'Rapid Transit for Toronto,' address to the Empire Club of Canada, 20 October 1949 (Toronto: The Empire Club of Canada, 1950).

13 Allan Lamport, chairman of the Toronto Transit Commission from 1955 to 1958, 'Planning for Transportation in the Metropolitan Community,' address to the Empire Club of Canada, 22 January 1959 (Toronto: The Empire Club of Canada, 1959).
14 *The Municipality of Metropolitan Toronto Act* (1953) states that all undertakings, assets, real and personal property belonging to the Toronto Transportation Commission are vested in the Toronto Transit Commission. The legislation also transferred all the liabilities to the new commission. Under sections 37 and 62, the statute vested the locally owned waterworks and trunk water supply lines as well as sewage treatment facilities and sewage mains to the Metropolitan government.
15 Metropolitan Toronto Planning Board, *Metropolitan Toronto 1953–1963* (brochure prepared for the Metropolitan Council, 1963).
16 *Toronto Star*, 'Brand Raps TTC Fare-Raise Plan: "Cutting services to show profits"' (3 February 1962).
17 *Toronto Transit Commission Annual Report*, 1967. In 1960 every one of the TTC's city transit routes made money; twenty-two suburban routes lost money.
18 Lawrence Solomon, *Energy Shock* (New York: Doubleday, 1980).
19 H.W. Tate, assistant general manager, Toronto Transportation Commission, in 'Rapid Transit for Toronto,' address to the Empire Club of Canada, 20 October 1949 (Toronto: The Empire Club of Canada, 1950). 'In the maximum hour between 5 and 6 o'clock we have to carry between 13,000 and 14,000 people north on Yonge Street, the heaviest travelled street car line in North America. In fact, we carry on Yonge Street in the rush hour more people than are carried in the maximum hour on one of the Boston subway systems operated by surface car.'
20 Of the 16.5 miles that constitute this segment of the subway, about ten miles were located within the city and three miles each were in the suburbs of Etobicoke and Scarborough.

2. Living at Close Quarters

1 New York's proportion was highest in 1910, at 40 per cent, compared to Toronto's 38 per cent and 36 per cent for both Chicago and Boston. By 1930, New York's immigrant share had fallen to 33 per cent, Boston's to 29 per cent and Chicago's to 25 percent, while Toronto's had held steady. Richard Harris, *Unplanned Suburbs: Toronto's American Tragedy, 1900 to 1950* (Baltimore: Johns Hopkins University Press 1996).
2 P.H. Bryce, chief medical officer of the Department of the Interior, Ottawa,

'Civic Responsibility and the Increase of Immigration,' address before the Empire Club of Canada, 31 January 1907 (Toronto: Empire Club of Canada, 1910).
3 'Your Home, Our City: 100 Years of Public Control over Private Space' (City of Toronto Archives, 2001).
4 Harris, *Unplanned Suburbs*, p. 174.
5 Ibid., p. 270.
6 J.M.S. Careless, *Toronto to 1918: An Illustrated History* (Toronto: James Lorimer, 1984). St John's Ward (or the Ward as it was popularly known) was located in a distinct area bounded by Yonge Street, University Avenue (Avenue Road), and King and College streets. More than 70 per cent owned by absentee landlords before the First World War, it now houses a hospital district.
7 With the leaseholds that were then common, landlords didn't own the land on which houses were built, leading to payments of 'ground rent' to the landowner.
8 Toronto outlawed wood-frame construction on the grounds that it would lower the risk of fires. Manhattan, in contrast, only banned wood-frame houses in its densest areas, and other cities permitted wood-frame houses but minimized the fire risk through changes in attic design and other innovations. Ironically, most Toronto houses today are built of wood.
9 Bryce, 'Civic Responsibility.' Although many perceived immigrants to rely on relief, Bryce provided statistics to demonstrate that relief was a minor problem. 'I have told you that there were 52,000 people came into Ontario last year, and, of course, Toronto is the great distributing point. I think, if I am not mistaken, Mr. Taylor reported that the total number of cases in 1906 which applied to the City Hall Office for relief was 1,026. That includes everybody, as I understand it, who came from any part of the population in Toronto, so that, so far as the actual relief goes, whether it was done by others or not, those are the figures. It is quite clear that on the relief side the matter has mended.'
10 Rosemary Donegan, *Spadina Avenue* (Vancouver: Douglas and McIntyre, 1985). Jews were prominent in the garment industry, Toronto's largest industry, and as grocers, particularly in serving the dietary needs of Toronto's large Jewish community.
11 Jews tended to take longer to acquire their own homes than other immigrants, due to a greater investment in their children's education. British immigrants, for whom home ownership was a paramount goal, encouraged their children to leave school at 14 and earlier in order to enter the workforce.

12 Robert F. Harney, *Polyphony*, vol. 6, *Chiaroscuro: Italians in Toronto, 1815–1915* (Toronto: Multicultural History Society of Ontario, 1984).
13 The second highest rate was Baltimore's, at 46 per cent. The median rate among the twenty largest cities was 30 per cent. New York's rate was 13 per cent and Montreal's 16 per cent.
14 New York City's density was lower at 18,800 people per square mile than Toronto's 20,200 but Lower Manhattan, and older parts of Boston and Chicago, had greater densities than any part of Toronto, which had a more even development, and much less undeveloped land than New York City. See Harris, *Unplanned Suburbs*, p. 38.
15 At Queen and Sherbourne Streets.
16 Canada Mortgage and Housing Corporation (CMHC), *Pro-Home: A Progressive, Planned Approach to Affordable Home Ownership* (April 2002).
17 In 'Civic Responsibility,' Bryce described the nature of regulations that did exist: 'Our building by-law is a remarkably good by-law, in nearly all respects ... if you will look into the particulars of that City building by-law with regard to the strength of buildings, materials and the kind of drainage that is required, the kind of house on a certain sized piece of land that is required, the impossibility of putting up houses on lanes less than 30 feet in width, you will find that all these things indicate that those who drew up the by-law have done a great deal to improve the tenement house condition of the City.'
18 Tom Cruickshank and John de Visser, *Old Toronto Homes* (Toronto: Firefly Books, 2003).
19 CMHC, *Pro-Home: A Progressive, Planned Approach to Affordable Home Ownership*, and economist James Mavor both estimated 25 per cent; Harris, in *Unplanned Suburbs*, provided the higher estimate.

3. Toronto the Good

1 The Alexandria later became an apartment hotel. See Richard Dennis and Ceinwen Giles, Department of Geography, University College London, 'Modernity and Multi-Storey Living: Apartment Tenants in Canadian Cities, 1900–1939.'
2 Richard Harris, *Unplanned Suburbs: Toronto's American Tragedy, 1900 to 1950* (Baltimore: Johns Hopkins University Press, 1996), p. 91.
3 Richard Dennis, Department of Geography, University College, London, 'The Regulation of Apartment Housing: Evidence and Speculation from Toronto and London,' September 2002. The city's first attempt to restrict apartment buildings involved Spadina Court, built in 1905 at the southeast

corner of Spadina and Lowther. It was thrown out of court, in part because the city did not have authority to regulate apartment buildings.
4 Peter Moore, 'Zoning and Neighbourhood Change in the Annex in Toronto' (PhD thesis, University of Toronto, 1978).
5 Small apartment buildings were built especially in the suburbs in the late 1920s, after Toronto regulations banned small apartment builders in much of the city. The city's bylaw did not apply in Forest Hill and York Township. See 'Your Home, Our City: 100 Years of Public Control over Private Space' (City of Toronto Archives, 2001).
6 The judge decided that the bylaw had been passed in bad faith, as 'an indirect attempt to regulate the building of apartment houses under the guise of regulating the distance of buildings from the street line, the power of regulating the building of apartment houses not having been conferred upon the Municipality, indeed having been expressly refused.' See Dennis, 'The Regulation of Apartment Housing.'
7 H.H. Williams to Toronto City Council, 15 January 1912.
8 'The fear was that apartment buildings would lower neighbouring property values, especially of single-family dwellings, presumably because of their physical bulk, potential traffic congestion and the presence of non-traditional family groups (such as groups of single sharers or unmarried cohabiting couples).' See Dennis and Giles, 'Modernity and Multi-Storey Living.'
9 Carolyn Strange, *Toronto's Girl Problem: The Perils and Pleasures of the City, 1880–1930* (Toronto: University of Toronto Press, 1995), pp. 128–9.
10 W. Struthers, a prominent public health official, cites numerous ills in warning 'the prevalence of venereal and other diseases are rapidly producing a degenerate race,' while Charles Hodgetts, a medical officer of health, feared the 'overcrowded permanent homes of a foreign population – hot beds of parasitic and communicable diseases and breeders of vice and inequity.' See Sean Purdy, 'Industrial Efficiency, Social Order and Moral Purity: Housing Reform Thought in English Canada, 1900–1950,' *Urban History Review* 26 (March 1997).
11 P.H. Bryce, Chief Medical Officer of the Department of the Interior, Ottawa, in 'Civic Responsibility and the Increase of Immigration,' address to the Empire Club of Canada, 31 January 1907 (Toronto: Empire Club of Canada, 1910).
12 The vices include prostitution, alcoholism, child neglect and incest, irreligion and Sabbath-breaking, thriftlessness, swearing, stealing, and 'love of finery' (a wickedness. associated with loose women who liked to dress up).
13 Hastings, a leading reformer, was the city's chief medical office of health

from 1910 to 1929. He had lost an infant daughter to milk-spread typhoid fever, which spurred his personal crusade of disease prevention. During his tenure, the Toronto Public Health Department became recognized internationally as a leading innovative and model department. He was president of Canadian Public Health Association in 1914 and 1916 and of the American Public Health Association in 1918.

14 Jamie Benidickson, 'Ontario Water Quality, Public Health, and the Law, 1880–1930,' in G. Blaine Baker and Jim Phillips, eds, *Essays in the History of Canadian Law in Honour of R.C.B. Risk* (Toronto: Osgoode Society for Legal History, 1999). See also Purdy in 'Industrial Efficiency, Social Order and Moral Purity:' 'Charles Hastings sent out women sanitary inspectors to go into immigrant's houses to "teach them how to clean up and keep clean their homes and environments ... Many of these people, by reason of birth and environments, have neither the moral stamina or the intellect to rid themselves of their vices and shortcomings."'

15 As described in Baltimore in 1895 by a Canadian clergyman at a prominent Purity Congress, social purity work in Canada included prostitution, divorce, illegitimacy, 'Indians and Chinese,' public education, suppression of obscene literature, rescue of fallen women, and shelters for women and children. See Mariana Valverde, *The Age of Light, Soap, and Water: Moral Reform in English Canada, 1885–1925* (Toronto: McClelland and Stewart, 1991), p. 17.

16 'Your Home, Our City: 100 Years of Public Control over Private Space,' City of Toronto Archives.

17 Toronto Mayor W.H. Howland stated that, in one lodging house alone, 'hundreds of children have been ruined.' See Valverde, *The Age of Light, Soap, and Water*, p. 136.

18 The cost of a washbasin and toilet in 1914 was $145 in 1914, according to city records, and $336 in 1921. Small houses sometimes cost less. In 1912 Hastings had 'found 8,000 unsanitary houses ... 4500 houses overcrowded as tenements ... surrounded by dirty foul-smelling undrained stables; manure heaps ... evil-smelling privies.' Hastings also demolished over 15,000 outhouses.

19 The demolitions that took place had the effect of forcing people into the suburbs, but it did nothing to improve their sanitation. In 1921, Richard Harris estimated, 'rather more than half of the population of Toronto's suburbs' lacked sanitation. In 1927, Canadian planner A.G. Dalzell estimated, 'over 50,000 people had settled in urban communities around the city of Toronto before any sewer construction took place.'

20 Moore, 'Zoning and Neighbourhood Change.'

4. Model People, Model Suburbs

1 J.M.S. Careless, *Toronto to 1918: An Illustrated History* (Toronto: James Lorimer, 1984).
2 Edwin Chadwick's 1842 report, *The Sanitary Conditions of the Labouring Population* (London) found that disease was directly related to living conditions.
3 Col. Edward Ackroyd created early model villages to house his employees at Copley (1849–1853) and Ackroyden (1859). Sir Titus Salt created Saltaire (1853–1863) at the site of his Alpaca Wool spinning and weaving mill in West Yorkshire. Prices Patent Candles built a model village around 1853. Lever, whose financial empire stemmed from the success of Sunlight soap, built Port Sunlight (1890) on the west bank of the River Mersey.
4 'Your Home, Our City: 100 Years of Public Control over Private Space' (City of Toronto Archives, 2001). See also Careless, *Toronto to 1918*, p. 193. The act also established a City Surveyor's Office to administer the measure.
5 Toronto City Council Minutes, 12 April 1912.
6 Adams became one of the world's foremost planners, and the most influential planner in Canada. He was one of the founders and first president of the British Town Planning Institute, a founder of the Town Planning Institution of Canada (forerunner of the Canadian Institute of Planners), a founding member of the American City Planning Institute (forerunner of the American Institute of Planners) and the force behind the creation of Canada's Civic Improvement League, among other achievements. He produced New York's first regional plan and effectively drafted legislation that would be adopted across the country.
7 Thomas Adams, town planning adviser, Commission of Conservation, 'Town Planning, Housing and Public Health,' report of the seventh annual meeting held at Ottawa, 18–19 January 1916.
8 To support agriculture and other rural industries, Adams argued for 'facilities and assistance in creating rural industries in small towns and villages and the other things which are necessary in combination to secure the successful settlement of land. These things are not beyond our reach, but they require us to pay the price demanded *ab initio*, in nearly every successful enterprise ... it will probably be found essential for government support to be given to start the schemes, both in the form of some financial credit and in the form of administrative energy. See Thomas Adams, 'Present Scope for Practical Work in Improving Civic Conditions,' Conference of Civic Improvement League of Canada, held in cooperation with the Commission of Conservation, Ottawa, 10 January 1916.

94   Notes to pages 34–9

9 Dr C.A. Hodgetts, medical adviser of the Public Health Committee of the Commission of Conservation, report of the third annual meeting of the Commission of Conservation in Ottawa, 1912.
10 The prescription included: 'The district for factories should be on the opposite side of the town to that from which the prevailing winds come, and these should accessible by both rail and water communication. The warehousing district should be placed convenient to the factories, the business offices, in the centre of the town where the land is dear.

 Public offices should be located in commanding positions, not only for the sake of the time and money saved to the public by the convenience of their positions, but because they should be dignified reminders of the corporation's [municipality's] existence, and act as inspirations to the patriotism of the people.'
11 'Housing and Town Planning,' presented by C.A. Hodgetts, medical adviser of the Public Health Committee of the Commission of Conservation, at the report of the third annual meeting of the Commission of Conservation in Ottawa, 1912.
12 Ibid.
13 'Present Scope for Practical Work in Improving Civic Conditions.'
14 Careless, *Toronto to 1918*, p. 179.
15 Spruce Court was Canada's first limited dividend housing project. See 'Housing Progress,' Appendix A, key event chronology.
16 Spruce Court now operates as a city housing co-op.
17 Richard Harris, *Unplanned Suburbs: Toronto's American Tragedy, 1900 to 1950* (Baltimore: Johns Hopkins University Press, 1996). In the 1940s another 18 per cent would be converted.
18 See Sean Purdy, 'Industrial Efficiency, Social Order and Moral Purity: Housing Reform Thought in English Canada, 1900–1950,' *Urban History Review* 26 (March 1997). Carver espoused efficient community planning to 'promote loyalty to local government, churches, recreation centres, institutions.'
19 Herbert A Bruce, 'Civilization and the Cave Man,' an address before the Empire Club of Canada, 18 March 1937 (Toronto: The Empire Club of Canada, 1937).
20 The Standard of Housing Bylaw led to federal home-improvement loans legislation making it easier for owners to repair or rebuild. By 1939, more than nine thousand homes had been inspected, with over half subsequently renovated or replaced. See 'Your Home, Our City: 100 Years of Public Control over Private Space.'
21 Bruce, 'Civilization and the Cave Man.'
22 Purdy, 'Industrial Efficiency, Social Order and Moral Purity.'
23 Bruce proposed a program of slum clearance and reconstruction using

Moss Park as a case study. His scheme – new row houses and low-rise apartments around a large central playground and other open spaces – would materialize after the Second World War as Regent Park North.
24 CMHC, *Pro-Home: A Progressive, Planned Approach To Affordable Home Ownership* (April 2002).

5. Canada's War Effort against the Cities

1 In 1916 there were 168 strikes involving 26,971 strikers; in 1917, 222 strikes and 50,327 strikers; in 1918, 305 strikes and 82,573 strikers; in 1919, 428 strikes and 149,309 strikers; and in 1920, 459 strikes and 76,624 strikers. See Canadian Museum of Civilization. Between 1916 and 1920, 350,000 people struck – half the workers employed in manufacturing, metal trades, shipbuilding, and clothing and textiles.
2 Rosemary Donegan, *Spadina Avenue* (Vancouver: Douglas and McIntyre, 1985), pp. 156–7. The Broadway Hall event on 1 May 1918 was large enough to warrant speakers for afternoon and evening rallies.
3 Cited by Sean Purdy in 'Industrial Efficiency, Social Order and Moral Purity: Housing Reform Thought in English Canada, 1900–1950,' *Urban History Review* 26 (March 1997).
4 Canadian Forces Advisory Council, *The Origins and Evolution of Veterans Benefits in Canada, 1914–2004* (Ottawa: Veterans Affairs Canada, 2004). The act was revised two years later and renamed the *Soldier Settlement Act: An Act to Assist Returned Soldiers in Settling upon the Land*.
5 The grants provided free land, except where returning servicemen already held a farm of average size, or received financial grants to assist them to acquire or maintain land.
6 2 September 1920, p. 2.
7 The acquisition of lands from Native people was controversial; Native people seek redress to this day for what they believe to have been a forced expropriation without fair compensation.
8 The act states: '2. Settlement areas shall be established only in districts wherein by reason of lands remaining undeveloped agricultural production is being retarded. 3. The Board shall be sole judge as to whether or not in any district, by reason of lands remaining undeveloped, agricultural production is being retarded, and the fact of the establishment of a settlement area in manner by this Part provided shall be conclusive proof in any court or otherwise that any lands within such area which the Board, pursuant to the following provisions of this Part, may proceed to purchase compulsorily are compulsorily purchaseable hereunder.'
9 Richard Harris and Tricia Shulist, 'Canada's Reluctant Housing Program:

The Veterans' Land Act, 1942–75,' *Canadian Historical Review* 82, no. 2 (June 2001). In addition to the attempt to settle veterans on the farm, the government, under a different program, attempted to provide suburban housing for veterans via a cost-sharing plan with municipalities. This effort also failed, with the exception of some red-brick row housing built in Rosedale. See David B. Mansur, *A Sense of Mission* (CMHC).

10 To add insult to injury, the *Veterans Land Act* denied Native people who fought in the war access to land otherwise made available to veterans: 'There is considerable injustice in the fact that while Indian land was being coveted to settle returning Canadian veterans, Indian veterans were not even being accommodated in the drafting of a new *Veterans' Land Act* (VLA). The IAB sent out a circular on 3 March 1945: "It is a matter of regret that no commitment of a positive nature can be made to Indian returned men at this time."'

11 *An Act to Assist War Veterans to Settle upon the Land, Statutes of Canada* (S.C.) 1942–43, c. 33, preamble.

12 It was assumed that most applicants would have 'limited agricultural experience,' that their wages would be of 'critical' importance, and that they would commute to an urban centre. See Harris and Shulist, 'Canada's Reluctant Housing Program.'

13 Ibid.

14 This provision would backfire, an outcome most drafters did not anticipate. Murchison thought that most beneficiaries would be urbanites, despite strong survey evidence to the contrary.

15 The act offered agricultural training and the opportunity for veterans to purchase 'land and improvements there-on, building materials, livestock and farm equipment up to a total cost to the Director of six thousand dollars.' Of the $6,000 loan, $2,320 was forgivable, with the balance payable over 25 years at the low interest rate of 3.5 per cent per annum. Title to all property remained in the hands of the director of the Veterans Land Administration until the loan was paid off, although the director had the authority to transfer title to livestock or farm equipment if he deemed it advisable. The plan accommodated commercial fishing on a similar basis.

16 *Globe and Mail*, 31 October 1944. The advertisements, published under the authority of Hon. Ian A. Mackenzie, minister of pensions and national health, were part of a series designed to 'inform the people of Canada of plans to re-establish men and women of the armed forces.' The series invited readers to obtain a booklet entitled 'Back to Civil Life.' More than one million copies of the booklet were distributed.

17 Initially, in April 1941, when the drafters saw the *Veterans Land Act* chiefly

in terms of full-time farmers, the committee predicted that 25,000 veterans would require assistance to reestablish themselves in farming. Over time, the administrators recognized that the act's small-holdings component had great appeal. By mid-1946, Murchison had quadrupled the figure to 100,000. Ultimately, small holders would outnumber full-time farmers by a ratio of more than three to one. See Harris and Shulist, 'Canada's Reluctant Housing Program.'
18 Canadian War Museum, Government of Canada.
19 In Ontario, the following figures applied: full-time farmers, 12.1 per cent; small-holders, 87.5 per cent; commercial fishermen, 0.1 per cent; settlers on crown land, 0.2 per cent. In Harris and Shulist, 'Canada's Reluctant Housing Program.'
20 Richard Harris and Tricia Shulist, '"Build Your Own Home": State-Assisted Self-Help Housing in Canada, 1942–75,' School of Geography and Geology, McMaster University, Ontario.
21 This committee controlled construction for all government programs.
22 At first, VLA administrators laid out their own subdivisions and entered into agreements with local builders. Because of cost overruns, and poor building quality, they bent to demands from veterans who wanted to build their own housing and soon developed a 'build-your-own-home' policy which offered various forms of technical assistance, including construction courses together with on-site inspections and guidance. By the mid-1950s, about 90 per cent of homes were owner-built, up from 28 per cent in 1946.
23 In 1945 Murchison reported that the subdivision scheme was 'intensely popular' and was already 'threatening to become the major part' of VLA activity. It was clear that the 'strong appeal' of the small holdings were 'as a means of obtaining a home,' not farm acreage. In 1946, while the half-acre provision was still temporarily in force, three-fifths of all applications were for this minimum, and doubtless many would have been happy with even less.
24 October 1945. Presented by Dominion president Alex Walker.
25 *Hansard*, 1 August 1946.
26 Howe controlled, among other organizations, the Department of Reconstruction and the CMHC.
27 In 1940 the government did briefly consider urban housing, when the General Advisory Committee on Reconstruction asked its subcommittee on land settlement to consider it. This request was soon dismissed, partly because giving veterans the choice of an urban residence posed a 'danger' to the greater objective of creating self-sufficient farmers, and partly because the *National Housing Act* already made home ownership available on 'easy terms.'

28 MP Frank Leonard, who had been on every veterans affairs subcommittee since 1935, stated that he had received 'more complaints about this one regulation than with regard to anything [else] concerning veterans affairs.' See Harris and Shulist, 'Canada's Reluctant Housing Program.'
29 As a result of opposition to two-acre lots, which the government saw as a bulwark against urbanization, the government agreed to a discretionary allowance of 20 per cent that lowered the actual minimum to 1.6 acres. By 1954 about half the smallholdings were of two acres or less; barely a fifth were of five acres or more.
30 In total, the *Veterans Land Act* financed 102,025 small holdings. The small holdings provisions of the act, though not meant to be a housing program, would house more people than Wartime Housing.
31 J.G.C. Herwig of the Legion and the British Empire Service League was almost alone in understanding the provisions' significance. He observed that 'the small holding feature will be the most popular [aspect of the *Veterans Land Act*] and will probably require the most careful administration.'
32 *Hansard*, 29 April 1999.

6. CMHC and Cheap Financing Open Up the Suburbs

1 Legislation in 1944 paved the way for the CMHC's creation. CMHC's offices opened 1 January 1946, at the Bank of Canada.
2 David B. Mansur, *A Sense of Mission* (CMHC). Dr McIntosh was Bill McIntosh, the acting deputy minister of finance.
3 To alleviate the shortage, the city government took several steps: It built some emergency shelter for the munitions workers within the city boundaries, it reversed regulations that had discouraged lodging, it established a room registry, and it exhorted householders to take in war workers. After the war, the city reverted to form. It discouraged migrants by taking out ads in Toronto newspapers to warn about housing shortages. Likewise, the federal government in 1944 forbid Canadians from moving without permission to various cities, which were considered to be overcrowded. The cities on the banned list included Victoria, Vancouver, Hamilton, and Ottawa as well as Toronto.
4 'Your Home, Our City: 100 Years of Public Control over Private Space' (City of Toronto Archives, 2001).
5 'Dominion Plan Seen Creating More Duplexes,' and 'Would Aid Kind of Servicemen by Converting Rosedale Homes,' *Globe and Mail*, 28 August 1942.
6 Some were attending university with the help of their veterans' credits, and they were billeted in army huts moved to the campuses of nine universities.

7 The Wartime Housing Corporation, created in 1941, also helped repair and modernize thousands of existing units. See CMHC, *History of CMHC*. Wartime Housing's Veterans Rental Housing program created about half of the corporation's 50,000 units.
8 This was CMHC's first major foray into real estate sales. The sales occurred over five years, beginning in 1950.
9 The federal government had provided mortgage insurance as well as joint mortgage loans through approved institutional lenders under the *Dominion Housing Act* of 1935, and later the *National Housing Act* of 1938. But because of financing costs and high minimum standards, NHA loans were unaffordable to most veterans, and remained so after the Second World War, when the CMHC took over this function.
10 The federal government's entry into the mortgage business would have another large consequence as well. The government required government-financed houses to conform to minimum standards, leading the Association of Canadian Fire Marshals to draw up a 'uniform building code for the entire Dominion.' After the war, codes were introduced and systematized in many suburban areas. Richard Harris, *Unplanned Suburbs: Toronto's American Tragedy, 1900 to 1950* (Baltimore: Johns Hopkins University Press, 1996), p. 156. Harris traces the regulations to Thomas Adams's 1918 report on housing for the federal government that led to the financing of local housing commissions and recommended 'model by-laws relating to building and sanitation.'
11 'In Danforth-Woodbine Park, for example, lots were initially priced at between $15 and $30 a front foot in 1912 and made available on 'easy payments': $50 down and $5 a month.' See ibid.
12 Jean-Claude Villiard, president, Canada Mortgage and Housing Corporation, in a 2001 speech entitled 'The Canadian System of Housing Finance: Past, Present and Future.'
13 The 1935 legislation provided financing on about 1,600 units per year. Enhanced 1938 legislation financed 3,600 units per year and even more liberal 1944 legislation provided financing on about 21,400 housing units per year. 'And in doing so, the 1944 legislation had created a national market for home loans that was more accessible to the borrowers and more viable to the lenders.' See ibid.
14 *The Labour Gazette*, February 1938.
15 The act led to '125,720 loans for modernization of existing homes, totaling nearly $50 million, on which the net loss represents a percentage of .806.' Paper by Royal Bank of Canada, November 1944, Montreal.
16 A 'house-conscious' feeling has been developed among Canadians which tends to promote character and citizenship. See F.W. Nicolls, director of

housing, Division of Finance, *Housing In Canada, 1938*, Housing Yearbook 1938 (Chicago: National Association of Housing Officials, 1938). The Home Improvement Plan, as with other government programs of that era, had a moral purpose: to 'upgrade' housekeeping and promote sturdy family life. See Margaret Hobbs and Ruth Roach Pierson, '"A Kitchen That Wastes No Steps ...": Gender, Class and the Home Improvement Plan, 1936–1940,' in Jeff Keshan, ed., *Age of Contention* (Toronto: Harcourt Brace, 1997).
17 Total residential construction in Canada for the year 1937 amounted to $56,200,000. Approximately 20 per cent of this amount was financed under the *Dominion Housing Act* with another 20 per cent made under the Home Improvement Plan. See Nicolls, *Housing in Canada*.
18 Mansur, *A Sense of Mission*.
19 Villiard, 'The Canadian System of Housing Finance.'
20 This innovation became one of the corporation's proudest accomplishments, according to David Mansur: 'During my time at CMHC, the Corporation made two outstanding contributions to the development of housing in Canada. One of them was direct lending – mortgage loans made directly by CMHC to house buyers and builders.'
21 The chartered banks, which held most of the national long-term savings, were prohibited by the *Bank Act* from making residential mortgage loans. According to Mansur: 'On October 1, 1953, Mr. St. Laurent announced that the changes [to the Bank Act] would be made. I had earlier made a deal with the Bank of Montreal, which were CMHC's bankers. They agreed that, if the changes were introduced, they would come to the party. So, on October 2, the day after Mr. St. Laurent's announcement, every newspaper in Canada had an advertisement saying that the Bank of Montreal was making 217 loans in Pointe Claire, Quebec. The other banks were not enthusiastic about the idea, but they were afraid of being left behind by the Bank of Montreal.'
22 Marsha J. Courchane, Freddie Mac, and Judith A. Giles, 'A Comparison of U.S. and Canadian Residential Mortgage Markets,' Department of Economics, University of Victoria. The insurance is available for both new homes and existing units, though initially it was only for new homes. Currently, a loan-to-value ratio of 75 per cent is the cutoff for the requirement for default insurance (compared to the 80 per cent cutoff in the United States).
23 Villiard, 'The Canadian System of Housing Finance: Past, Present and Future.'
24 'Your Home, Our City: 100 Years of Public Control over Private Space.'
25 David Dunkelman, *Your Guide to Toronto Neighbourhoods* (Toronto: Maple Tree Publishing, 1999).

Notes to pages 55–7 101

26 This description appears in the Canadian Enterprises Gallery of the Canadian Heritage Gallery, a housing industry website that CMHC co-sponsors.
27 Mansur, *A Sense of Mission*.
28 In a survey of twenty developed countries, Canada had rates of home ownership that were seven to 22 percentage points greater than most. Marsha J. Courchane, Freddie Mac, and Judith A. Giles, 'A Comparison of U.S. and Canadian Residential Mortgage Markets,' Department of Economics, University of Victoria, 2002.

7. Partial Amalgamation, Full Sprawl

1 This estimate of 100,000 is conservative. In Ontario 42,394 veterans took advantage of the *Veterans Land Act*'s small-holdings program, perhaps 40 to 50 per cent of them settling in the Toronto region. During the baby boom, the average fertility of women in Canada rose to 3.9 children, implying households of close to six people, plus members of the extended family. Suburban families exceeded the Canadian average in size and suburban homes often housed lodgers as well. Assuming that the homes built under the smallholdings program housed six people in the postwar years, and that 40 per cent settled in the Toronto area, the *Veterans Land Act* directly established a suburban population of 102,000 in the Toronto region. In addition, the 102,000 would have attracted tradesmen, retailers, and other service providers, further increasing the smallholdings program's importance in populating Toronto's outskirts.
2 The government of Ontario (and to a lesser extent, Toronto) augmented federal efforts. Chapter 8 describes Ontario's role.
3 Civic Advisory Council of Toronto, First Report, Section 2, of the Committee on Metropolitan Problems, 1950. See also, *Report of Municipal Statistics* (Province of Ontario, 1953).
4 Gore and Storrie, Consulting Engineers, 'Report on Water Supply and Sewage Disposal for the City of Toronto and Related Areas,' 15 September 1949.
5 Jacob Spelt, *Toronto* (Toronto: Collier-Macmillan, 1973), p. 85.
6 Patricia Hart, *A History of the Borough of North York* (Toronto: General Publishing, 1968), p. 272
7 James Lemon, *Toronto since 1918, An Illustrated History* (Toronto: James Lorimer, 1985), p. 111.
8 Toronto Transit Commission, *TTC Story: Transit in Toronto* (Toronto: The Commission, 1969).
9 Lemon, *Toronto since 1918*, p. 108; H. Carl Goldenberg, *Report of the Royal*

Commission on Metropolitan Toronto (Toronto: Government of Ontario, June 1965), p. 39. The ratio of elementary school pupils per 100 residents in Toronto was 9.7 while in the outer suburbs this ratio ranged from 18.4 to 19.2 or double that in Toronto. Similarly, the taxable assessment in Toronto per student was about double that in the outer suburban municipalities.

10 Frederick G. Gardiner, address to the Empire Club of Canada, 5 November 1953 (Toronto: The Empire Club Foundation, 1954).
11 In 1946, 90 per cent of the manufacturing enterprises in York County were still within the boundaries of the City of Toronto. By 1954 that figure fell to 77 per cent as businesses migrated to former agricultural land beyond the city limits. Carl Benn, *The History of Toronto: An 11,000 Year Journey* (Toronto: City of Toronto Culture Division, 2006), www.toronto.ca/culture/history.htm accessed 19 November 06.
12 Gardiner, address to the Empire Club, 5 November 1953.
13 Province of Ontario, *Annual Report of Municipal Statistics*, 1953.
14 Goldenberg, *Report of the Royal Commission on Metropolitan Toronto*. Civic Advisory Council of Toronto, First Report, Section 1, of the Committee on Metropolitan Problems, 1949, pp. 34–5.
15 David Estrin and John Swaigen, *Environment on Trial* (Canadian Institute for Environmental Law and Policy) (Toronto: Emond Montgomery Publications, 1993). The pollution of streams was an offence under riparian law; pollution of groundwater fell under nuisance law.
16 Timothy J. Colton, *Big Daddy, Frederick G. Gardiner and the Building of Metropolitan Toronto* (Toronto: University of Toronto Press, 1980), p. 63. Petty politics, as well as lack of money, also prevented the growth of the region, Gardiner felt. He lamented to Premier Leslie Frost that there was 'such a persistent demand to retain local autonomy, local taxing powers and local administrative powers as to make one despair of any cooperative effort which will solve the problems that are common to the area.'
17 The suburbs of Long Branch, New Toronto, and Mimico had applied to be amalgamated, while another proposal had the amalgamation of Etobicoke, Long Branch, Mimico, and New Toronto. The Town of Mimico also applied for a board of management. See 'Amalgamation vs. Cumming Plan,' an address to the Empire Club of Canada by Controller Leslie H. Saunders, 25 February 1953 (Toronto: The Empire Club Foundation, 1953).
18 Gardiner, address to the Empire Club of Canada, 5 November 1953.
19 Frederick G. Gardiner, in testimony to the Ontario Municipal Board, *In the Matter of the Application of the City of Toronto Pursuant to Section 23 of the Municipal Act*: 'So we tried, in the colloquial terms of the Planning Board, to

"pinch" that highway through so as to get it up [through] the metropolitan area. And the Township of York told us they did not want it. No use going through all the arguments again unless you want some development of it. They simply did not want it.' Colton, *Big Daddy.*
20 City of Toronto Archives, *The History of Toronto.* The history adds: 'These needs became imperative with the post-war population explosion and its attendant housing shortages and rapid development of the areas around the city.'
21 'The second basic form of administrative set-up that offers for the solution of the problem involves the unification of local governing bodies into one central administration. Such a system is free from the many shortcomings and disadvantages of the Commission method or Borough System as noted above. It cannot only assure the most efficient carrying out of all the matters that might be entrusted to any Commission, Board of Management or Metropolitan Council but can also control that most important question of land use, the neglect of which is the basic cause of all municipal difficulties.' Premier Frost's statement, reported in Board of Control report, described in 'Amalgamation vs. Cumming Plan, An Address by Controller Leslie H. Saunders.'
22 'The Metropolitan Problem,' address by Eric Hardy (Toronto: The Empire Club of Canada, 1950).
23 'Amalgamation vs. Cumming Plan.' The decision to seek amalgamation was overwhelmingly passed by city council, 17 to 2.
24 'Eleven of the twelve suburban municipalities righteously and indignantly defended their local autonomy. In the face of such violent opposition the Ontario Municipal Board concluded that it was not advisable arbitrarily to force the eleven opposing municipalities into one amalgamated municipality. On the other hand it recognized that the dangers inherent in the situation required early and effective action and recommended that the Province of Ontario pass legislation to establish a metropolitan system of municipal government for the whole area.' Frederick G. Gardiner, Chairman of the Municipality of Metropolitan Toronto, in 'Metropolitan Toronto,' address to the Empire Club of Canada, 5 November 1953.
25 *Municipality of Metropolitan Toronto Act*, 1953, sections 37 and 61. The legislation established a two-tier system: In addition to the existing local government tier, a new Metro-wide tier was created to provide various services on a Metro-wide basis.
26 Lemon, *Toronto since 1918.*
27 *Toronto Telegram*, 22 January 1953.

28 The capacity of the existing Ashbridge's Bay facility was enlarged.
29 'Metropolitan Toronto Planning Board,' document produced for Metropolitan Toronto Council, July 1967.
30 Ibid., brochures produced for Metropolitan Toronto Council, July 1963 and July 1967. See also 'Toronto's Water Supply Systems' from the City of Toronto website: www.city.toronto.on.ca/water/history.htm.
31 Described in chapter 1.
32 In 1967, under the new system, the city's contribution to Metro's public school funding pool amounted to 42 per cent while its population fell to 36 per cent of Metro's. See 'Financial Profile of Metropolitan Toronto and its Constituent Municipalities' (Background Report prepared for the Royal Commission on Metropolitan Toronto, Government of Ontario, 1976). In 1986 when the city's population was 30 per cent of Metro's, it contributed 40.4 per cent towards the Metro school system. See Francis Frisken, 'Planning and Servicing in the Greater Toronto Area: The Interplay of Provincial and Municipal Interests' (Urban Studies Working Paper Series, York University, 1990), p. 20.
33 Colton, *Big Daddy*, p. 113. Gardiner was a leader of the progressive wing of the Ontario Progressive Conservative party, an ardent advocate of moving the party away from its traditional conservative positions. Former prime minister Arthur Meighen, a Conservative, dubbed him 'Social Security Gardiner' for his views. Not shy about planning on a large scale, in 1945 Gardiner told the *Toronto Star* that the province needed 'something in the nature of Joe Stalin's five-year plan' to deal with hospital construction.
34 The assessment base formula applied to most but not all infrastructure. Taxable assessment refers to the total assessed value of the properties in a municipality. Properties owned by churches and educational institutions, for example, were exempt.
35 Government planners considered the redistribution from the city to the suburb highly equitable in that it reduced disparity in service levels among various parts of the metropolitan area. However, from another point of view, this sort of redistribution was far from equitable. Despite the city's rich tax base, its residents were poorer than the suburbanites they were subsidizing. According to the 1961 census, the average family income of Toronto residents was $5,594 and the average income in the suburban communities receiving the subsidy ranged from $6,518 in Scarborough to $7,680 in Etobicoke. Neither was the central city without needs of its own. It was burdened by ageing and deteriorating neighbourhoods as well as large pockets of slum housing. About half of the neighbourhoods, mostly in the southern part of the city, were in the process of decline and another

32 per cent were vulnerable. There was concern about depreciation of property values and increased flight of the well-to-do residents to the suburbs, coupled with anxiety about decreasing assessment as well as increased public expenditure on relief. See City of Toronto Planning Board, Third Report, 1944.
36 Goldenberg, *Report of the Royal Commission on Metropolitan Toronto*, p. 132. The city's 62 per cent share of Metro's capital subsidy for new schools in 1954 dropped to 39 per cent in 1963. The funding formula excluded until 1964 the cost of rehabilitating old school buildings, denying the city during Metro's first eleven years money to upgrade existing school buildings, many of which were in disrepair.
37 Sydney Hermant (member of Metropolitan Toronto Planning Board), 'Metropolitan Toronto – Planners Dilemma,' address to the Empire Club of Canada, 11 January 1968, (Toronto: The Empire Club Foundation, 1968). In the mid-1960s, the average selling price of a home in Canada was $17,400 (CMHC).
38 Rather than basing charges on the cost of delivering the service, for example by considering the amount of pipeline and other capital required to provide services to low density areas, the utility charged a uniform rate based on volume of water supplied to finance its waterworks' capital and operating expenses.
39 Goldenberg, *Report of the Royal Commission on Metropolitan Toronto*, p. 40. Residents in the other neighbouring municipalities were buying water from Toronto (and New Toronto, which also produced its own water) at a rate of 13 cents to 24 cents. For the two producing municipalities water works had been a source of profit.
40 Eric Hardy, 'Submission to the Royal Commission,' on behalf of the City of Toronto, 16 March 1964, p. 17.
41 Described in chapter 1.
42 Goldenberg, *Report of the Royal Commission on Metropolitan Toronto*.
43 Hardy, 'Submission to the Royal Commission,' p. 12.
44 Mike Filey, *The TTC Story: The First Seventy-Five Years* (Toronto: Dundurn Press, 1996).
45 Of the metropolitan council's twenty-five members, twelve represented city residents, twelve suburban municipalities, with the Metro chair appointed by the province. Thus the city, with 57 per cent of the population and 62 per cent of its tax base, had fewer than half of the votes. Because the city needed votes from suburbs, it was forced into making deals with suburbs to avoid votes along strict city-suburban lines.
46 Metropolitan Toronto Planning Board, 'Key Facts,' April 1970, Table 11. In

the same 1954 to 1967 period, the city's population grew marginally to 685,000.
47 Despite these results, Metro became 'the most admired and "reproduced" system of regional government in the world.' See Betsy Donald, 'Spinning Toronto's Golden Age: The Making of a "City That Worked,"' *Environment and Planning* (2002).
48 Under 1966 provincial legislation, the number of representatives from suburban municipalities increased to twenty, in a new thirty-three-member council.
49 Toronto Alderman Tony O'Donohue provided background testimony to the provincial legislature's Standing Committee on General Government: 'Goldenberg had just brought in his report on Metropolitan Toronto. It was the first review since the formation of Metro in 1953. His recommendations led to more power for the Metro government. It also gave political control to the suburban members for the first time. This alarmed city politicians. They planned to do something about it. Metro must not be allowed to dominate.

A plan was formulated to fight for total amalgamation. At the first opportunity, which was the municipal election of 1969, Toronto city council placed the amalgamation question on the ballot. We thought that a solid Yes vote would convince Premier John Robarts that amalgamation was the solution ... Generally the people knew that an efficient and understandable one level of local government with less bureaucracy was what they wanted. It was not a hard sell during that election. When the ballots were read, 101,163 voted yes and 22,390 voted no, 82% in favour of amalgamation. But that went nowhere, as the Premier turned it all down' (*Hansard*, 20 February 1997).
50 Toronto throughout its history has refrained from developing its lands and it still has much undeveloped and underdeveloped land, including along its extensive waterfront. Various cities that have expanded their boundaries since 1950 have retained substantial amounts of undeveloped land, among them Winnipeg. Even New York, which experienced a major amalgamation more than a century ago, in 1950 still had substantial amounts of undeveloped land in the boroughs of Queens and Richmond.
51 Metro's population increased a mere 5 per cent between 1971 and 1985.
52 Metropolitan Toronto Planning Board, 'Key Facts,' July 1986.

8. The Suburbs beyond the Suburbs

1 A 1949 Department of Highways Traffic Survey estimated that 'a potential volume of approximately 10,000 vehicles per day would use this facility

when constructed.' By 1956, when the Toronto Bypass was completed, the department estimated 48,000 vehicles per day.
2 In 1971 and 1972 Highway 400, which had been designed with the limited purpose of linking Barrie to Toronto, was widened to accommodate interchanges to Bradford, north of Toronto. In 1982 the province extended the Don Valley Parkway beyond the Toronto boundaries to Aurora and Newmarket, to the northwest of Toronto.
3 'Toronto Area Transit Operating Authority Annual Reports,' March 1979 and March 1994.
4 In 1972 the provincial government's new Ministry of Environment absorbed the OWRC.
5 Ontario Sewer and Water Construction Association, 'Drinking Water Management in Ontario: A Brief History,' submission to the Walkerton Inquiry, January 2001.
6 Darcy McKeough, 'Where the Action Is,' address to the Empire Club of Canada, 20 March 1969 (Toronto: The Empire Club Foundation, 1969). 'The crisis in the municipalities has been building up for many years, and government action has built up accordingly. We have introduced a variety of measures. For the most part, these have been grants, subsidies and other forms of financial support. The Province now pays nearly half the cost of the services and functions that are administered by local authorities. In other words, the local bodies collect only a little over half their budgets through local taxes; the rest of the money is raised by the Province from its broader tax sources.'
7 Margaret Beare, 'The History and the Future of the Politics of Policing,' Sociology and Law, Osgoode Hall Law School, 2004.
8 Robarts had first presented his plan, Design for Development, in the Ontario legislature four years earlier.
9 'I foresee a larger role being played by government in all our lives in the years that lie ahead. I cannot say I am particularly happy about this because I am not happy about the intrusion of government into our private lives. Nonetheless, I do not see any other way that we can deal with the many extremely large problems which face our people today ... It will require that some individual rights take second place to the rights of the group, because as our population increases and these matters become more complex, the group has to be considered to an extent that the group has not been considered, perhaps, heretofore. We may have to ask that the people submerge some of their positions as individuals in the interests of long-range planning and in the interests of establishing a proper and fitting place for their children and grandchildren.' 'The Road to Reform – Ontario

Style,' address by John P. Robarts, Prime Minister of Ontario, to the Empire Club of Canada, 9 April 1970 (Toronto: The Empire Club Foundation, 1970).
10 William R. Allen, Metro's chair, described Toronto's excesses in a 1965 speech: 'The metropolis, as a cluster of cities, towns, villages and formerly rural townships, will grind to a halt, unable to produce that which its citizens require unless there is a form of area municipal government to be contrasted with the isolated, solitary, almost self-sufficient municipality of the 1800's.

This exemplified itself in the Metropolitan Toronto area, a cluster of thirteen municipalities which had been fully exposed to the present century concentration of population, in the form of internal competition for available money to be loaned, an inability to co-ordinate planning in any way so that the city proper burst at the seams and the overflow was growing up "like Topsy"; water rationing; septic tanks; public transportation available only in the city with various private lines servicing the twelve other municipalities; traffic stagnation – remember the little bridge over the Humber at the western gateway to Toronto, the Eglinton Avenue of that day which terminated in the east at Victoria Park, the Sunday night jams in Hogg's Hollow?

It was the combination and cumulative effect of all these situations which led to the creation of a metropolitan, or regional, or area municipal government for this metropolis.' See 'The New Toronto' (Toronto: The Empire Club Foundation, 1966).
11 'One of the major problems facing the big cities of the world is the question of fragmented local government, where it is not possible to get things done on a broad basis. So against the wishes of certain people, Mr. Frost [former premier Leslie Frost], you did what you did. We are all duly grateful that you did this in Metro the way you did it. We are going to hope for the same type of thing in our regional development program.' 'The Road to Reform – Ontario Style,' address to the Empire Club of Canada by John P. Robarts, Prime Minister of Ontario, 9 April 1970 (Toronto: The Empire Club Foundation, 1970).
12 Ministry of Treasury, Economics and Intergovernmental Affairs, 'Proposal for Local Government Reform in an Area East of Metro' (December 1972). As in Metropolitan Toronto, the region-wide municipalities – Halton, Peel, York, and Durham – were responsible for regional services such as arterial roads, trunk sewers, water mains, sewage treatment, water filtration facilities, police and regional planning. Local services such as fire protection, local roads, local planning, and zoning remained with the lower tier. By the

1970s, the province had created twelve regional municipalities, four of them in the Toronto area.
13 Ibid., 'Regional Government in Perspective: A Financial Review' (Staff paper, 1975).
14 Metropolitan Toronto Planning Department, 'Key Facts' (May 1995).
15 Even so, Robarts's political party, the Ontario Progressive Conservatives, would pay an electoral price at the polls. The regional municipalities proved to be unpopular, despite the subsidies.
16 These included the Parkway Belt West Plan (1973), the Niagara Escarpment Plan (started in the 1960s but approved in 1985), and, most recently, the provincial government introduced Smart Growth plans in the 1990s, a new Greenbelt Protection Plan in 2004, and, in 2006, the Growth Plan for the Greater Golden Horseshoe, to be implemented over twenty-five years.
17 They also constituted a hefty 40 per cent inside Metro. See Ministry of Treasury, Economics and Intergovernmental Affairs, 'Regional Government in Perspective: A Financial Review.'
18 In 1996, according to the Greater Toronto Area Task Force report, education 'accounts for at least 55 percent and as much as 70 percent of property taxes collected in different parts of the GTA.'
19 Greater Toronto Area Task Force, 'Greater Toronto' (January 1996). The provincial education grant was designed to equalize the ability of school boards to spend on education regardless of the municipality's assessment base. Because a school board's assessment base is directly related to the market value of all the property in the municipality, municipalities with valuable land and buildings generate more revenues for school boards than communities with low-value properties. The provincial grant to school boards make up the difference between a school board's needs and the amount of property tax revenues it raises. Thus municipalities with large tax bases receive smaller per-pupil grants than those with smaller tax bases. The grants were based on a tax-assessment formula that made Toronto schools ineligible for grants (Submission to the GTA Task Force by the Regional Board of Durham, Halton, Peel and York). The suburban municipalities received these provincial grants although their residents were often better off than Torontonians: Based on the 1991 national census, Toronto's average household income was $54,249 while that of suburban Oakville, served by the Halton District School Board, was $77,253. Yet the Halton school board received $1,483 per student in 1993 while Toronto's received nothing. In effect, the province subsidized the more affluent people in a low-density suburb and not those less well-off in higher density Metro.

20 Ibid.
21 June Rowland, 'Conflict or Cooperation: The Toronto-Centred Region in the 1980s' (Symposium held at York University, March 1982).
22 This education tax rate varies across the province, with Toronto's tax rate well exceeding that of the other GTA regional municipalities. In 2001 Toronto commercial property owners paid 2.65 per cent of the assessed value of their property in educational property taxes, while in Halton commercial properties paid 1.8 per cent and in Durham 1.9 per cent. The average for the 905 regions was 2 per cent. Because of this higher tax rate, and because Toronto properties tend to be more valuable than those outside the city, Toronto businesses in 2001 paid $1,018 more towards the cost of educating each pupil than Halton businesses and $2,003 more than businesses in Durham (Ontario Ministry of Education, *Parent's Guide to Student-Focused Funding*; *Financial Statements for the year 2001*: Toronto District School Board, Halton District School Board and Durham District School Board). This pattern of subsidies continued after Ontario government reforms in 1998 that saw the province set and receive a provincial property tax for education, and then provide school boards with a flat per-student education grant to cover expenses that, in the province's judgement, should be met. See Ministry of Education and Training, 'News Release' (13 January 1997).
23 Density is defined as the ratio of the city's population to its total area.
24 Demographia, *Toronto: Population, Area & Density by Sub Area: 1996*. www.demographic.com. Accessed 13 May 2006.
25 IBI Group, *Greater Toronto Area Urban Structure Study*, Summary Report, prepared for the Greater Toronto Coordinating Committee, June 1990, Exhibit no. 2: 'GTA Structure Concepts: Overview of Population and Employment Distribution by Region.'

Conclusion

1 'To the West, I have made a preliminary proposal for regional government in the Counties of Peel and Halton. You will recall that a review of the local government structure in this area was completed two years ago. However, we could not accept the recommendations of this review because it called for a distinct separation of the area into two regions – one rural and one urban. Our view is that the division of urban and rural economies is a method of the past. My proposal suggests one regional government covering both counties and a small part of Dufferin County around Orangeville.' Darcy McKeough, 'Where the Action Is,' address to the Empire Club of Canada (Toronto: The Empire Club Foundation, 1969).

2 'Suburbanites live there by choice. The majority of people want a greener, more spread out low-density development with lots of space for their children to play. People also enjoy driving their cars, which is the preferred choice of more than 70% of Torontonians.' James Alcock et al., *Environment History and Planning of Toronto in the 20th Century*.
3 S.D. Clark, *The Suburban Society* (Toronto: University of Toronto Press, 1966).
4 Patricia Hart, *Pioneering in North York: A History of the Borough* (1968). In the era that Hart describes, before the influx of immigrants, 'North York had been a community of Methodists, almost entirely.'
5 Ibid.
6 Even Levitttown, the iconic U.S. suburb that epitomized the suburb's success, did so by overcoming the distaste that the general public felt for the suburb: 'We are ending the old bugaboo about uniformity,' Levitt said in announcing a new suburb. 'In the new Levittown we build all the different houses ... right next to each other in the same section.' See Lawrence Solomon, *Energy Shock* (New York: Doubleday, 1980). On another occasion, Levitt boasted 'the least monotonous mass housing group in the country.' He made his name by selling homes on the cheap, often without basic amenities and mostly to buyers with Veterans Administration financing. To appeal to budget buyers, Levitt built early homes without basements and used bamboo screens rather than wood in closet doors.
7 Early in Canada's history, governments were especially intent on colonizing the continent, and so provided incentives for homesteading and other pioneering pursuits. Many governments favoured resource exploitation over secondary or tertiary industries. From Thomas Jefferson on, the continent had an ethic that discouraged urban life.
8 Metro Chairman Alan Tonks reflected on Metro's success in managing change in 1966. 'We had an effective mechanism to anticipate change, and manage it in an orderly and remarkably undisruptive manner. This maintained social stability in our region. It set us apart from so many American cities, catapulted us onto the world stage and gave us a competitive edge in the global economy. The Boston Consulting Group's study for the GTA Task Force confirmed that the Toronto area is attractive because of its quality of life and social stability. This is a safe place in the league of big cities. We have managed to draw strength from the diversity of our population rather than let it tear us apart.

Metro managed to protect and nurture one of the most vibrant central cities in North America. Just compare what has happened to the City of Toronto with what has happened to its American central city counterparts

over the past 40 years.' Allan Tonks, Chairman, Metropolitan Toronto Council, 'The Future of the Greater Toronto Area,' address to the Empire Club of Canada, 25 January 1996 (Toronto: The Empire Club Foundation, 1996).
9 In Cabbagetown families not only 'doubled up' but 'tripled up,' leading Hugh Garner, in the preface to his novel *Cabbagetown*, to call it 'a sociological phenomenon, the largest Anglo-Saxon slum in North America.' This high-density area, which 'had for some time been singled out as a dangerous "slum,"' became the target of housing reformers. Regent Park, today the epitome of the slum, was initially lauded by the *Toronto Daily Star* as 'Heaven.' See Sean Purdy, '"Ripped Off" By the System: Housing Policy, Poverty, and Territorial Stigmatization in Regent Park Housing Project, 1951–1991,' *Labour/le Travail* (2003).
10 Richard Harris and Robert Lewis, 'How the Past Matters: North American Cities in the Twentieth Century,' *Journal of Urban Affairs* (1998).
11 Greenwich Village has a population density of about 60,000 per square mile, New York's West Side and Upper West Side about 100,000.

Postscript

1 The province's Greater Toronto Area (GTA) Task Force, mandated to make recommendations on a wide range of matters including governance of the GTA, in its final report in January 1996, recommended the elimination of the Metro and regional governments and the establishment of a GTA authority. The subsequent Who Does What Panel, established by the province and chaired by David Crombie, recommended the creation of a Greater Toronto Services Board, elimination of the regional municipalities and consolidation of member municipalities into strong cities, including a strong urban core for the GTA.
2 UK Transport Secretary Alistair Darling, in a 9 June 2005 speech to the Social Market Foundation, formally presented the government's intention. Universal road pricing had also been part of the Labour Party's election manifesto.
3 Because peak demand creates the need for additional road capacity, the capital costs of a road tend to be allocated to peak users. Other costs associated with road use, such as wear and tear, are allocated on the basis of the weight and type of vehicle. Some road pricing schemes also allocate environmental costs to users.
4 Transit vehicles might come at a frequency of once an hour rather than once every twenty minutes; residents might be required to bring their own garbage to the dump.

5 Since the property tax was first introduced in Ontario in 1793, it has taken several forms, among them the inclusion of personal property, which incorporated an income component.
6 'Vital Signs 2005,' Toronto Community Foundation, www.tcf.ca. Accessed 26 November 2006. Toronto is following the trend of other cities in expelling its middle class. In 2000, 56 per cent of Toronto households were middle class, compared with 63 per cent in 1980. Meanwhile, the number of low-income households grew from 18 per cent to 22 per cent and high-income rose from 19 to 22 per cent.
7 In the 1902–12 decade, for example, blue-collar workers occupied 80 per cent of new suburban homes in Toronto.
8 Myriad other rules discriminate against high-density developments. They include requirements that apartments include kitchens, which needlessly raise the cost of downtown living for those who prefer to frequent neighbourhood restaurants for their meals (such apartments were once common), requirements that housing developments include parking, even in areas well served by public transit, and bans on subdividing properties.
9 Jeffrey J. Cantos, 'Parking Strategies for Affordable Housing: An Efficient and Equitable Approach,' a report prepared for the agency Let's Build, City of Toronto, 2004.
10 For example, City of Toronto By-law No. 950–2005, enacted October 28, 2005: 'To enact a new City of Toronto Zoning By-law with respect to lands east of Warden Avenue north and south of St. Clair Avenue, to be known as the Warden Woods Community.' The density measure here is the gross floor area, which excludes certain uses such as mechanical rooms.
11 The Greater Toronto Area produces 50 per cent more farm output than Nova Scotia, 67 per cent more than Prince Edward Island, and 80 per cent more than New Brunswick.

Index

Adams, Thomas 33–5, 86, 93
Age of Light, Soap, and Water 27
Ajax 55, 67
Alexandria 23, 90
Allen Expressway 61
Allen, William R. 15, 108
amalgamations 3, 7, 8, 56, 58–60, 63, 65, 66, 69, 71, 77, 79, 86, 102, 103, 106; partial 56–65, 69, 77, 79
American Public Health Association 92
Annex, the 21, 22, 24, 77
annexations 6, 7, 86. *See also* amalgamations
apartments 21, 23, 24, 26–8, 32, 76, 82, 90, 91, 95, 113
Association of Canadian Fire Marshals 99
Aurora 67, 107
automobile 12, 14, 16, 81; and congestion 79–80 112; and sprawl xi–xii, 58–62, 66, 111

Baltimore 90, 92
Bank Act 100
Bank of Canada 52, 98
Bank of Montreal 100

Beaches, the 76
Beck, Adam 5, 10, 87
Belgium 34
Belt Line. *See* Toronto Belt Line Corporation
Bennett, R.B. 37
Board of Control 24, 67
Board of Inquiry into the Cost of Living 20
Board of Management 102, 103
Board of Social and Moral Reform of the Presbyterian Church 25
Board of Trade 10
Boston 88, 90
Boston Consulting Group 111
Brampton 67
Bruce, Herbert A. 37–9, 94
Bryce, Peter H. 17–20, 26, 89, 90
Bureau of Municipal Research 60

Cabbagetown 28, 36, 76, 112
Canada Mortgage and Housing Corporation. *See* CMHC
Canadian Architect and Builder 24
Canadian Legion 43, 47
Canadian Manufacturers Association 41

Canadian Public Health
    Association 92
*Canadian Soldier's Handbook of General
    Information* 45
Carver, Humphrey 37, 39, 94
Cavers, C.W. 42
Central Mortgage Bank 52–3
Chadderton, H. Clifford 49
Chadwick Report 31–2, 93
Chicago 19, 26–7, 88, 90
Cities and Suburbs Plans Act 32
City and Suburban Electric Railway
    Company 87
City Beautiful Movement 86
Civic Guild of Art 10, 86
Civic Improvement League 93
Clark, C.S. 6, 7
Clark, S.D. 73, 75
Clarke, C.K. 25
CMHC 40, 50–1, 53–6, 97, 100, 101
Coatsworth, Emerson 4
Commission of Conservation 33–5
Crerar, T.A. 43–4
Crombie, David 112

Dalzell, A.G. 92
Davenport Street Railway
    Company 87
Department of Defence 45
Department of Indian Affairs 43
Department of Reconstruction 97
Depression. *See* Great Depression
Design for Development 68, 107
Dinnick, Wilfred 18
Dominion Housing Act 38, 51–2, 99,
    100
Don Mills 75
Don River 3, 6, 9 57, 61, 107
Don Valley Parkway 107
Doukhobors 42

Drew, George 65
Dufferin County 110
Durham 67, 70, 71, 108, 110

East Toronto 9, 10
East York Township 86
Emergency Shelter Program 50
England, Robert 44
Etobicoke 14, 16, 52, 66, 71, 88, 102,
    104
Europe 76
European Union 79
*Federal Home Improvement Loans
    Guarantee Act* 52
First World War 7, 19, 20, 23, 29, 33,
    41, 42, 44, 87, 89
Forest Hill 7, 20, 23, 52, 58, 86,
    91
Frost, Leslie 60, 102, 103, 108

Garden Cities of To-morrow 32
Garden City 31–3
Gardiner, Frederick 57–9, 61, 63, 102,
    104
Gardiner Expressway 63
Garner, Hugh 112
General Advisory Committee on
    Demobilization and
    Rehabilitation 44
General Advisory Committee on
    Reconstruction 97
GO Transit 66, 71
Goldenberg, H. Carl 61, 62
Gore and Storrie 57
Grand Trunk Railway 11
Great Depression 7, 11, 23, 36–7, 45,
    50–52, 58
Greater Hydro 87
Greater Toronto 3–10, 12, 69, 71–2,
    77–9, 83, 109–13

Greater Toronto Area Task
  Force 109, 111–12
Greater Toronto Services Board 112
Greenbelt Protection Plan 109
Greenwich Village 77, 112
Gregg, Milton 44
Growth Plan for the Greater Golden
  Horseshoe 109

Halton 71, 108–10
Halton District School Board 109
Hamilton 85, 98
Hardy, Eric 60
Harris, Lawren 19
Harris, Richard 12, 19, 92, 99
Hart, Patricia 74–5, 111
Hastings, Charles 27–9, 91–2
Herwig, J.G.C. 98
High Park 6, 22, 77
Highway 401 66
Highway 407 70
Hodgetts, C.A. 34, 91
Holland 34
Home Improvement Plan 100
Housing Centre 39
Housing Commission 7, 29, 30, 32,
  36
Houston, William 10, 11, 86
Howard, Ebenezer 32
Howe, C.D. 48, 97
Howland, W.H. 92
Humber River 3, 10–11, 22, 57, 108
Hydro-Electric Power
  Commission 5, 87

Ilsley, J.L. 50
Indian Affairs Branch 43–4, 96
Industrial Canada 41
Interdepartmental Housing
  Committee 47

Jersey City 12
Junction 9, 19, 35, 76

Kidd, Thomas 47
Kingston Road Tramways
  Company 87

Lake Ontario 3, 58, 85
Lamport, Allan 14–15, 63, 67, 88
Lawrence Manor 54
Lawrence Park 18, 51
Lawrence Park Estates 18
Lawrence Plaza 54
Leaside 52
Leonard, Frank 98
Levitttown 111
lodgers 20, 26, 28–9, 30, 35, 37, 92,
  101
Long Branch 102
Looking Forward, Looking Back 43

Mackenzie, Ian A. 47–8, 96
Mackenzie, William 85, 87
Maclean, W.F. 3–6, 9–11
Manhattan 87, 89, 90
Mansur, David B. 50, 53, 55,
  100
market value assessment 80–1
Markham 64, 67
master plan (1943) 60
Mavor, James 19, 90
McIntosh, Bill 50, 98
McKeough, Darcy 67, 72
McLean, W.A. 19
Meighen, Arthur 42, 104
mergers. *See* amalgamations
Methodist Department of Evange-
  lism and Social Services 27
Metropolitan Street Railway
  Company 87

118 Index

Metropolitan Toronto 8, 13–16, 60–70, 88, 103, 106, 108
Milan 77
Mimico 87, 102
Mississauga 64, 67, 69
Montreal 4, 11, 41, 100
Montreal Park and Island Railway 11
Moral and Social Reform Council of Canada 25
Morality Department 25
Moss Park 21, 95
Municipal Act amendment (1921) 30
Municipality of Metropolitan Toronto. *See* Metropolitan Toronto
Municipality of Metropolitan Toronto Act 88
Murchison, W. Gordon 43, 45, 48, 96, 97

National Council of Veteran Associations in Canada 49
National Housing Act 48, 54, 55, 97, 99
New Brunswick 113
New York 12, 19, 27–8, 77, 87–8, 90, 93, 106, 112. *See also* Manhattan
Newmarket 67, 107
NHA. See *National Housing Act*
Niagara Escarpment Plan 109
Nicolls, F.W. 52
North Toronto 7, 10
North York 14, 56–8, 66, 71, 74, 75
Nova Scotia 113

Oakville 109
Ontario Bureau of Industry 25
Ontario Housing Committee 29
Ontario Hydro-Electric Commission 87

Ontario Municipal Board 60, 86, 103
Ontario Progressive Conservative Party 104, 109
Ontario Water Resources Commission 66, 107
Orangeville 110
Ottawa 17, 26, 98
OWRC. *See* Ontario Water Resources Commission
O'Donohue, Tony 106

Paris 77
Parkdale 6–7
Parkway Belt West Plan 109
Peel 71, 108, 110
Pickering 67
Pioneering in North York 74–5
Planning Act (1946) 65
Planning Board 57, 59, 65, 102
Porteous, Charles 11, 87
Prince Edward Island 113
Proud, George 49
Purity Congress 92

Regent Park 39, 65, 76, 95, 112
Richmond Hill 67
Riverdale Court 36
Robarts, John 67–9, 106–7
Rose, Albert 39
Rosedale 6, 21, 96
Rowlands, June 70
Royal Commission on the Relations of Labour and Capital 25
Rutherford, T.J. 48

Sanitary Conditions of the Labouring Population 93
Saskatchewan 42, 45
Scarborough 11, 14, 16, 52, 66, 71, 75, 88, 104

Seaton 6
Second World War xi, xii, 43–5, 51, 53, 65, 72–5, 82, 95, 99
shacktowns 18–19
Silverthorn Park 22
slums 19–20, 27, 31, 35, 37–9, 41, 104, 112; clearances 31, 35, 37–9, 65, 94
small holdings 44–9, 97–8, 101
Smart Growth plans 109
Social Service Congress of Canada 25
Soldier Settlement Act (1917) 42–4, 95
Soldier Settlement Board 42–4
Spadina Court 90
Spadina Heights 7, 86
Spadina Heights Residents' Association 86
Spadina subway 15–16
Special Committee on Veterans Affairs 47
Spruce Court 36, 94
St Alban's Ward 6
St George Mansions 23
St John's Ward. *See* Ward
St Laurent, Louis 100
St Paul's Ward 6
Standard of Housing Bylaw 38, 94
Standing Committee on National Defence and Veterans Affairs 49
Strange, Carolyn 25
Suburban Society 73
Swansea 86

tenements 19, 26–8, 90, 92. *See also* apartments
Tonks, Alan 111
Toronto and Hamilton Railroad Company 85
Toronto and Mimico Electric Railway and Light Company 87
Toronto and Scarboro' Electric Railway, Light and Power Company 87
Toronto and York Planning Board 57, 59
Toronto & York Radial Railway Company 87
Toronto and York Roads Commission 59
Toronto Belt Line Corporation 11
Toronto Board of Control 67
Toronto Co-Partnership Garden Suburbs Ltd 35
Toronto Gas Light and Water Company 85
Toronto Housing Commission 7, 29, 36
Toronto Housing Company 35, 36
Toronto Public Health Department 29, 92
Toronto Railway Company 12, 13, 87
Toronto Transit Commission. *See* TTC
Toronto's Girl Problem 25
transit: as a promoter of sprawl xii, 4–5, 9–16, 66, 71, 77, 81–7; regulation of 4, 8, 10, 12–16, 60, 63, 77, 79–81, 112; suburban 9–16 19, 36–7, 57, 59–61, 63, 66, 71, 77, 79–80, 88, 112; viability of 5, 9, 11–16, 59–61, 66, 71, 77, 80, 87, 112
TRC. *See* Toronto Railway Company
TTC 13–16, 57, 62, 63, 88

Union of Canadian Municipalities 4, 85
Union Station 16

United Kingdom 31, 79
United States 13–14, 21, 26, 68, 73, 76–7, 87, 93, 100, 111

Valverde, Mariana 27
Vancouver 98
Veterans Land Act (1942) 44–8, 50, 56, 96–8
Veterans Rental Housing 99
Victoria 98, 108
Villiard, Jean-Claude 53

Ward, the 6, 19, 20, 25, 36, 89

Wartime Housing Corporation 51, 98–9
Westmount 4
Who Does What Panel 112
Winnipeg 41, 42, 106
Winnipeg General Strike 42

York County 6, 59, 102
York Regional Municipality 70–1, 108
York Township 3, 7, 23, 86, 91, 103
Yorkville 3, 6, 7, 67
York-Durham pipeline 67, 70–1

The University of Toronto Centre for Public Management Monograph Series

The Klein Achievement / Barry Cooper

Expanding Horizons: Privatizing Post-Secondary Education / Douglas Auld

The McKenna Miracle: Myth or Reality? / William Milne

Cure or Disease: Private Health Insurance in Canada / Steven Globerman and Aidan Vining

How Ottawa Rewards Mediocrity / Fred Lazar

From Heartland to North-American Region State: The Social, Fiscal and Federal Evolution of Ontario / Thomas Courchene with Colin Telmer

The Federal Government and the Prairie Grain Sector: A Study of Over-Regulation / Colin Carter and Al Loyns

Reducing, Reusing and Recycling: Packaging Waste Management in Canada / Donald Dewees and Michael Hare

Past (In)Discretions: Canadian Federal and Provincial Fiscal Policy / Ronald Kneebone and Ken McKenzie

Governing in Post-Deficit Times: Alberta in the Klein Years / Barry Cooper and Mebs Kanji

Canada and Foreign Direct Investment: A Study of Determinants / A. Edward Safarian and Walid Hejazi

Liquid Assets: Privatizing and Regulating Canada's Water Utilities / Elizabeth Brubaker

Private Health Care in the OECD: A Canadian Perspective / Philippe Cyrenne

'If You Build It ...' Business, Government and Ontario's Electronic Toll Highway / Chandran Mylvaganam and Sandford Borins

The Economics of Genetically Modified Wheat / Colin Carter, Derek Berwald, and Al Loyns

Greener Pastures: Decentralizing the Regulation of Agricultural Pollution / Elizabeth Brubaker

Toronto Sprawls: A History / Lawrence Solomon